Praise for

DON'T KNOW MUCH ABOUT INDIANS
(but i wrote this book about us anyways)

First-time author Gyasi Ross has assembled a collection of his writings into a book that once opened, will be hard for any reader to put down. These are simple stories that pack a punch – sometimes gently, sometimes forcefully – and always with one foot planted firmly in the realities of life for Indian people today.

Tacoma Weekly

The work of Gyasi Ross hits you between the eyes. You're cruising along, reading his new...book.... You're thinking that the story or poem is going in one direction, when suddenly it takes a hairpin turn and you find yourself teetering on the edge of your initial set of conclusions, regaining your balance and reorienting your vision along with Ross's.

Indian Country Today Media Network

Buy this book; it's uplifting in its message of strength, native strength. It's enjoyable to read and reread. It will have you laughing, crying, but most of all, thinking.

Indianz.com

This little paperback book of stories and poems by Gyasi Ross is a gem. You will not find here lyrical trips into the past or the spiritual. Ross is all about confronting the present. He hits hard. ...the world of the book is rampant with stereotypes and abuses (of the body and the heart). It is also full of wistfulness, kindness, patience, and intelligence.

Wabquest.edublogs.org

Short stories and poems in the voice of the regular Joe Indian are a compelling representation of what it means to be a Native today.

Great Falls Tribune

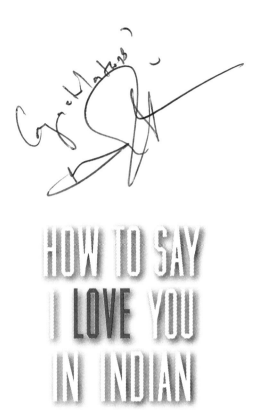

HOW TO SAY
I LOVE YOU
IN INDIAN

GYASI ROSS

Published by Cut Bank Creek Press
Printed in the United States of America

ISBN 978-0-9838118-1-7

Library of Congress Cataloging-in-Publication Data has been applied for.
For information about bulk purchases, contact:
cutbankcreekpress.com (North and South America)
gazellebookservices.co.uk (Europe, Asia, Africa)

This is a work of fiction. Apart from obvious historical references to public figures and events, all characters and incidents in this novel are the products of the author's imagination...the names have been changed to protect the innocent. Any similarities to people living or dead are purely coincidental.

Cover art by Steven Paul Judd. steve@restless-natives.com
Book design by Kim Pyle. k.m.pyle@comcast.net
Author Photograph by Anthony "Thosh" Collins. www.thoshography.com

TABLE OF CONTENTS

FOREWORD

OK. So I'm thinking to myself, why did Gyasi ask me to write for this book? I am not the role model in the romantic love sort of thing. Not for lack of trying. Let's say, maybe just unlucky. I dunno. A woman who loves her family, loves her community, loves her horses, loves her people and loves her land – all ferociously. Can women like me love a companion, a man, as well as all of the rest? And how does love work – the big love and the love between lovers? And, what I know for sure is that love maintains our faith, and faith maintains our love.

I was raised by a good family, and am raising six children, and let's say five or so grandchildren. Because of love. Yes, because of love. And because no child should be left. And because I believe in us, and am pretty sure that the only way that love works is if you put your *mana'o,* or your power, into it. But you have to hold your love close, and not let it fall into disrepair, dependency, sorrow or the gutter. Eh...

I love the testimony to love. I love a love that cares for families, making bread, fixing my car, washing clothes, and fighting battles all for love. I love the idea of understanding that we are a testimony to love, indeed, faith that we would still be here, and a faith that we will get through some of what we've been shackled with. I love young men who want to embody love and young women who know they deserve it, and want to nurture it. I love shaking off anger, frustration, low self-image, bad luck and trying love, again and again, because it is all worth it. I love the idea of a love which is forgiving, allows for redemption, and calls us to love with greater depth – our people, our companion, our children and our earth. I love that we are still here in all of our courage, and we don't give up on ourselves and on love. And I love this book.

Winona LaDuke
Round Lake Anishinaabe Akiing

INTRODUCTION AND
THANK YOUS

Love is survival. Love is about not going away even when you should, even when all signs tell you that you should go away and die. Logically, Native people should have died off a century ago, when great forces fought mightily and evilly to exterminate us from the U.S. consciousness.

But we didn't die off. We never know when to quit.

Native people know desperately clinging to life better than anybody else – we're like roaches, but in a good way. We survive circumstances that would have killed a less adaptive species. Love is survival. Ergo, Native people know love better than anybody else because we survive better than anybody else.

Makes sense, right? More on that later, though.

Before getting there, I want to tell you a couple quick and beautiful love stories that I know to be true; these are stories where real life was more beautiful and fantastic than fantasy. Indian stories. Desperate stories. Love stories – not all amorous, or romantic; love has many faces. Here are a few faces – humble Native men and women who loved deeply and powerfully and desperately.

Indian Women's Love

I have to start with women's love – mama's (and grandma's) boy that I am. Any discussion of Native love, Indian love has to start with women.

In my life, the love and sacrifice of Native women has constantly given me life and sustained me. My tiny, beautiful mom almost bled to death when she hatched me; my sister Neoma rescued me from drowning when I was three years old (and she was just a few years older than me) as I was being sucked down into the bottom of a lake; my sister Wendy beat up and protected me from the bullies who left me bloodied, bruised and feeling worthless in my pre-adolescence; my aunties Wanda and Wilma Faye and Cathy took me in when my maternal grandpa died and my mom was going through a very hard time and wasn't the mom that she usually was; my great-grandma Old Lady Singer taught me that elders will gladly pass on teachings and traditions if we just earnestly show interest, she opened up to me and trusted me with her precious Players cigarettes during Sundance; my aunties Leeta and Alfreda took me in when my dad got himself into a lot of trouble and I was homeless as a teenager; my cousin Dana taught me about girls and told me about not getting girls pregnant in my mid-teens; Bryna taught me that I was smarter than I thought I was and encouraged me to go to college; Miranda taught me that not everyone that I love will abandon me and made me trust her enough that we've spent a good portion of our adult lives together and had a beautiful baby together.

They all loved me and made sure that I ate and that I knew the difference between right and wrong – an awkward, pigeon-toed, very imperfect, mixed-breed, Indian boy.

Indian Men's Love

Indian men can love powerfully. In my studies and experience, Native men have every single bit of capacity to love as beautifully and healthily and powerfully as Native women – and that's saying a lot. I've observed and heard so many beautiful stories, many within my own family. I think of my maternal grandfather, Percy Bullchild, despondent at his wife's (my grandma's) cervical cancer diagnosis. Therefore, this Native man – with five little kids in tow – literally goes all over the country and Canada trying to get his wife healed. Desperate, not wanting to lose the love of his life, he goes to every single traditional healer he can find, he goes to every evangelical healer that he can find. Heck, he even tracked down Oral Roberts and paid a substantial sum of money to that charlatan so that he might work to heal my grandpa's beloved wife.

She died. He was distraught. In pain. He wanted to give up. This traditional Blackfeet man's faith in the Creator that he served so diligently was put to the test. Yet he persisted – his Indianness wouldn't let him give up – and began making a different kind of love story. He raised his five children by himself as a single father (until he later married the beautiful woman that I know as my grandma,

Rose). He also raised a generation of pow-wow singers and dancers, showing his love of his Native culture.

He survived not because of, but to, love.

I also think of my good friend Peter Joe. Peter was from the Huu-ay-aht First Nation of Vancouver Island told me about how he literally canoed across the Salish Sea on his way to find his love, Gerri. That's not an easy pull. But like my grandpa Percy, Peter's love didn't stop there; his romantic love was only a small piece of the love for Native people that he showed during his life. He also raised five children, and was also there to give us young punks grandfatherly advice anytime we needed it. I was always amazed at Peter's energy – he would joke around with me as if he were a little kid. Childlike. He always made me feel important, as he did most folks around him. In fact, his life's work was making homeless Natives feel important and valued as he passed out free lunches and took inventory of our homeless brothers' and sisters' needs every single day.

I think of these two Native men – they didn't run from their responsibilities. They didn't have children all over the place for women to take care of. They didn't beat their wives.

And that forces me to rethink my prejudices; just because MY experiences with Native men might have been underwhelming, doesn't mean that there aren't incredible Native men out there. There are. I had to get over myself and realize that one experience doesn't speak for all experiences. But more on that later.

Combined, these short stories about Indian women and Indian men make me think of Native peoples' capacity to love. It's amazing. You look at our history and you realize that genocide and daily assaults on our self-esteem, physical safety and food supplies were not enough to destroy the love that we had for each other. We would not die – we probably should've died, but we wouldn't. We stayed alive because of love. The reasonable response to the realization that "we're dying and there's nothing that we can do about it" is to give up. Native people, and specifically Native women, would not allow us to do that. They held us together – imperfectly, with bungee cords and bubble gum – yet, still they held our communities together.

Those Native women and men knew the solution; they loved harder. It's not like they wanted to – they had no choice!!! It was either love harder, or Native people cease to exist.

It's so easy to love when everything is going well. When my son does well, for example, of course I reward him and tell him how proud of him I am. That's easy. However, when he breaks a window or goes to jail or acts ungrateful, that's when the love is put to the test. Similarly, most people simply haven't had the tests on their love that Native people have – Indian parents having their children snatched away, Indian women having their fallopian tubes forcibly ligated, Indian men being told that they cannot support their families because they choose to live on their homelands where unemployment is many times the national average. That's when love is tested. That's when people stop believing. God is picking on you, there is no God...!!!!!

...there is no...love....

Somehow, we didn't go down that road. Somehow, we continued to believe and love.

Love is not a soft or sentimental thing. Love sets rules. Love demands and draws lines in sand. Love creates expectations. It says, **"My love doesn't have conditions but it does have expectations."** Oftentimes, people confuse the two – that having unconditional love means that you fall for anything. No. That is not love. Love is putting up strict and strong rules for your children, "You will not play close to the street. I don't care how bad you want to." Love is the motivation – we want our children to survive and thrive. Love motivates us to take a hard line, "I will not allow alcohol in this house. We are not going to repeat history." That hard line helps our children to do better.

Love is taking the time and discomfort to talk, honestly, about an addiction that is killing a loved one. It would be very easy to let that loved one slip down into a pit of self-destruction and pretend that you do not see them slipping into that pit. Only love – non-judgmental yet honest – will require you to help them crawl out. There are many of us who would rather pretend that we don't see something – that is not love, because pretending that we don't see self-destructive behavior doesn't help anybody survive.

Love is survival. Love is the singular reason that our people still exist, despite genocide. Love is the reason that Jewish people still exist, despite the ugliness and pain of the Holocaust. Love is the reason that African-Americans still exist as a people, despite the horrible crime of American slavery. True love is resilient. Native love is the most resilient of all – after all, 500 years of resistance to extermination, disease, murder, rape and plunder is a very long time.

The motivation behind this book was simply to acknowledge Native peoples' amazing capacity to love. All Native people – enrolled or not; it doesn't matter your mixture, upbringing, or geographic location. All blends of Natives come from that powerful legacy of enduring love – from the full-blood Lakota in Rosebud, to the teenager who was raised white in Oklahoma and just discovered that she was part Native, to the African-American man in Washington D.C. who simply knows that he's "got some Indian in him" because his family always respectfully acknowledged that history[1] – you are here because of Native love. Be proud – you come from strong and loving people. Our love is not perfect, by any stretch of the imagination; no one's love is perfect. But we continue to love, to believe, to have faith and to look toward the future of our people. That is remarkable. Yet, very few people have felt compelled to remark about it. Let me explain:

I was at a wonderful tribal college looking at their impressive library. Beautiful library, literally thousands of Native-themed titles; I'd never seen anything like it. I spent a couple of hours there – I was there to speak at the school and was killing time, taking in the lovely campus – just perusing the aisles of the impressive library. There was an amazing array of subjects: Native spirituality, Native philosophy, law, economics, nutrition, art (this was, after all, Santa Fe), mathematics, history, etc.

Amazing.

But I don't think that I saw one book that discussed Native people's love directly. There were certainly books that involved or mentioned love – for example, Louis Erdrich's amazing "Love Medicine." But there were none that I saw where "love" was the central theme.

"That's a shame," I thought. "We have so much loving to be proud of because we have so much surviving to be proud of." Love is survival.

My cousin Robert Reevis and uncle Lyman Bullchild and uncle Gene Guardipee – all who passed into the next world within the past year – taught me a lot about the "survival" part of love. I wasn't raised around my dad that much, and so these three Native men took the time to have crucial conversations/give me spankings/make me feel loved when they didn't have to. They didn't just spank me, although they definitely did that when they needed to. They also hugged me. Made me feel valued. Spent special time with me.

And they make me think of healthy Native male love. Like Peter and Grandpa Percy.

Healthy love, not a militaristic approach to love that simply says "Native boys need discipline" and repeats the dysfunction of the whole boarding school, "beat the hell out of them" ethic. "Kill the Indian, save the man." My thought is more, "Love the Indian boy healthily, the man will happen." I'm a very insecure dad, always thinking that I'm somehow screwing my son up for life. That insecurity compels me to ask him, "How do you know that I love you?" He answers me, "Because you spend lots of time with me." I smile because I know that, in spite of my many flaws, shortcomings and imperfections, that is the right answer. His complete security and expectation that I'm supposed to spend time with him shows me that I'm doing something right.

We've got to spend lots of time with our Native children.

That investment of times allows us to show Native boys all the shades of love: disciplinary, affectionate, practical and physical. Teach them how to box/defend themselves and also how to braid their little brother's hair.

Native boys need healthy Native males to model healthy Native love (key word, "healthy"). We need to teach young Native boys to hold ourselves to a higher standard than the vast majority of the population does, non-Native AND Native – teach our kids to expect the world of us. **"Son/daughter, your love shouldn't have conditions but it should have expectations."** Native males get a bad rap – I started this section off by talking about all the Native females who did amazing things for me, and then, begrudgingly acknowledging the incredible Native males in my life. That's normal – like Chris Rock said, the only thing that dads can expect is the big piece of chicken. And yes, there are a LOT of Native males who screw up and leave children to be raised by their mothers and who don't financially provide for their children. That's a fact and I cannot dispute that. I'd like to dispute that, but I cannot. But I still contend that the thought that "there are no good Indian men" is a fallacy, an evil white supremacist myth that wants to demonize all men of color while ignoring the same behaviors in white men. Savages. Uncivilized. "Look, they can't even take care of their own kids." We can. I see plenty of "good Indian men"; there are undoubtedly those who need a lot of work, but there are those who are trying.

So here are my counterarguments to the "there are no good Indian men" fallacy:

My first counterargument is my Grandpa Percy and dear friend Peter Joe and all the many Native men like them – there's a whole bunch. I learn lessons from great young Native (and non-Native) fathers every day – Dallas, Charles, Coyote, Ryan, Rion, Dave, Chester, Rusty, Tatanka, Pat, Everett, Loren, Alan, and so on. They are the first counterargument to claims that Native men cannot be powerful and responsible family men and fathers.

My second counterargument to the "there are no good Indian men" fallacy is that, unfortunately EVERY race in the United States has a serious fatherlessness problem. It's not just Natives. Yet, it seems like many Native people (including me, many times) want to pretend like Natives have our own special brand of dysfunction. We don't – it's dysfunction that affects all of America. Just like everyone else in America, our families (unfortunately) were profoundly influenced by colonization, and one effect of colonization that Native men seemed to buy wholesale was that we can make little beautiful Native kids indiscriminately and not take care of them. That's never been Native peoples' way – our small communities held us accountable and punished deadbeat dads – but now we have admittedly acquired that attribute from the colonizer.

So we need to work on that. Definitely – Native women have held us together, in large part, for a very long time. We Native men need to get our shit together. But the theory that Native men are a special brand of deadbeat dad scumbag does not hold up statistically. That theory, I suspect, was created by White media to demonize men of color and Native men. What I mean by that is this: you rarely ever hear about the problems of fatherlessness within the White community even though there is a very serious problem with fatherlessness there. Disparate treatment. We should not fall into the White media's habit of making men of color and Native men look like animals. Love for our people compels that we should look at how to fix these problems for future generations. There are undoubtedly "good Indian men," just as there are "good Indian women." When Native people say that there aren't, I find that they usually have an agenda for saying so.[2]

Let's work on these relationships instead of simply pointing fingers. I definitely have a tendency to point fingers at us Native males – I was raised by superwomen – and tend to put Native women on a pedestal. But that does not help – nor is it honest. Accountability helps – at the same time Native men need to work on getting better and healthier, Native women also have to claim responsibility for not being patient and oftentimes knowingly choosing the least responsible Native men to have children with. No more "half-way" honesty; we all have responsibility – taking responsibility helps. Reconciling relationships helps. Finding out underlying reasons for dysfunctional behavior helps. Debunking bogus theories helps.

Therefore, my third response to the "Native men are scumbags" theory is NO, it is absolutely not Native women's job to build up the fragile and damaged self-esteem of us Native men. Not one bit. Yet, I submit that when Native women fall into the White media's habit of stereotyping Native men with such notions that there are no good Native men or that all Native men have kids everyplace

---

[2] When I hear these sorts of ignorant and absolute statements, "There are no good Indian men" or "There are no good Indian women" I instantly suspect that those making these blankets statements are implicitly justifying their desire to be with a Native person, so they damn all Indian men or women in the process. Obviously there is nothing wrong with a Native being with a non-Native person – love is love – but why not simply be honest about preferring another type of person instead of condemning an entire subset of Native people? "I prefer white/black men to Native men" or "I prefer blondes to Native women" is a much more honest AND correct statement than "There are no good Indian men/women."

or that Native men cannot/will not provide financial support, it is counterproductive to the health of a Native community. Not only is it factually inaccurate, but it is also self-fulfilling prophecy and will cause history to repeat itself.

Think about it.

"There are no good Native men."
"Native men have kids everyplace."
"Typical Native man."

When a young Native man hears those words from the women who gave him life and sustain him – his mom, his sisters, his aunties – think of what he suspects that his own course in life will be? "Well damn, I'm a young Native man and I suppose that I won't be good either."

When a young Native woman hears those words from their Native female elders, it stands to reason that the young lady will go into relationships with Native men with more baggage and suspicions than if she didn't hear those statements. That strikes me as not necessarily healthy for a relationship. History repeats itself, and while it's Native men's absolute obligation to model good behavior for younger Native men, it's also Native women's job not to repeat the destructive (and statistically inaccurate) lies of the White media and teach those precious young Native men that they are genetically predisposed to be bad or shiftless or jobless or an absentee dad. Instead of brainwashing our young Native men and boys to believe that they will never be good fathers, we should start trying to find ways to give them the tools to fix these vicious, learned cycles of fatherlessness and irresponsibility. When something goes wrong with our car, we don't talk about how this ONE CAR breaking down is conclusive proof that there are NO good cars out there, do we? No, we fix it (or buy a new car). Native children need strong and healthy examples of female love as well as strong and healthy examples of male love and sabotaging the work of the other doesn't help anybody.

Moreover, it is absolutely Native women's job to also take accountability for their choices in Native men they choose to allow into their lives. Just like any other race of men, not every Native man deserves to be a father, a husband, a partner or even a friend (or to further the "car" analogy, some cars are just pieces of junk and are beyond repair. Whose fault is it when a mechanic wastes time trying to fix the unfixable?). Native women must work and be patient-yet-stern enough to expect the world from their Native man – to demand good and chivalrous treatment. **"My love doesn't have conditions but it does have expectations."**

As much as I have a tendency to blame men for everything that goes wrong in a relationship (being raised by women will do that to you), honesty requires that I recognize that love is a two-way street. Responsibility and accountability goes both ways.

We know there are tons of amazing Native women out there. Tons. They are the backbones of our communities and families – they've always been there and will continue to be there. We must appreciate them, love them, and work hard to deserve those amazing Native women. But there are also plenty of Peters and Grandpa Percys out there – more than one might think. They're not perfect – none of us are. But we try pretty hard, try to be good fathers, try to be decent partners and co-parents; it's not perfect, but we're trying. We just need to be willing to recognize them and make Facebook memes and talk about them as much as we seem willing to do the same for the bad ones. The bad ones are out there, but so are the good ones. It behooves us to tell both sides of the story.

LET'S HEAR IT FOR THE GREAT

NATIVE DADS OUT THERE!

I think about healthy romantic love for Natives. This is another area where we have to be careful with the language and concepts we choose to put forth. Granted, Natives have some pretty dismal statistics when it comes to romantic relationships – bad numbers when it comes to divorces, fatherlessness, domestic violence, etc. Yet, so does everyone else. Plus, we have to acknowledge the role that economics and race play into love – most divorces happen because of financial problems. That's a fact. Native people come from some of the most depressed economies in the US – imagine the strain that lack of money has on Indian love. We've never been able to see how GOOD we could love each other if we didn't have to contend with the added strains of love and being broke!!! That's not an excuse – it's simply saying that we have to be honest and not make ourselves feel that we are fighting an unwinnable war to love.

We will win. Because love is survival, and when it comes down to it, nobody knows more about loving to survive than Native people.

This book is dedicated to those who are teaching me how to love, unconditionally: Mom, Miranda, Koodzi, Sutah, Manuel/dad, Wendy, Nomey, Willie/papa, John Ross – Ross Clan, Purcell Clan. Bouré Clan. Bullchild Clan. Bear Medicine Clan. Scabby Robe Clan. Eagle Speaker Clan. Old Person Clan. Dusty Bull Clan. Sharps. White Grass. All of Starr School. Belarde Clan. Lewis Clan. Deams, Old Coyotes, Franks, Spoonhunters, Tatseys, Murrays, Croffs, Beans, Ramirezes, Johns, McGimpseys, Gonzaleses, Powells, Gottfriedsons, Millers. Also, my Haskell Family, Blackfeet Community College, Seattle Central Community College, my Columbia Family. Mainly though, this is dedicated to my beautiful homelands – the Blackfeet Tribe, the Suquamish Tribe, the Puyallup Tribe, the Landing and Nisqually Tribes – without which I wouldn't have any of these stories. I love the places I come from, and am thankful for all the love that you've given me and kindnesses that you've shown me and my family.

Vanessar, Pat, Port Gamble Sklallam Tribe, Martin, Judd, Breezy, Marquise, Big Brothers Ernie, Brian C-Mr. President, David and Rion, Willie, Billy, Doc, Mow, Spap, Hank, Allison (RIP), Rit (my white philosophical dad), Mr. Harney, Sarah, Barson, BL, Reneezy, LJO, Niccola, Fleezy, Arlyn, Hank Adams, Lizzle, James, Wille, Doc, James, Ra, Oba, Dune, Wayne, Lenny, Big Chuck, Teek, Snizz, Patrick, Jazz, Ringo, Vince, Jess, Toni Gilham, Chi, Fredricka, White Chuck, Freddie, Kiese, Van, Dream, Bill Watterson, bell hooks,

John Mohawk, Darrell Kipp, Winona LaDuke, Greg Tate, and all my thinking/writing/loving heroes. I owe you all a lot. Thanks. My team, Cut Bank Creek Press – Michelle, Kim – you guys do amazing work and are incredible friends. Michelle, thank you for literally doing everything except writing this book.

Every Tribe. We do this for love – let's not confuse material gain with self-love and/or happiness. That's cool; we were given this system so I guess we have no choice but to do our best to make it work for us. But we must not ever think that it is ours or think that success in this system is victory for our people. It is just a tool. We are hunter-gatherers, tribal people, and let's work to remember that our happiness is inextricably linked to our mentoring and loving the younger generations and getting them ready to do the same for the generation under them. We cannot afford to forget that, otherwise we become just like everyone else and that kind of defeats the point. Native people are bigger than economic development, bigger than dysfunction, bigger than 500 years of oppression – this American experiment is only a small drop in the bucket of Native peoples' existence on this continent. The past 500 years does not define us; how we move forward from it will.

We have been here for tens of thousands of years and ONLY with love will be here for another thirty or forty thousand. Only with love. Our past is splattered with unconditional, inspired love that compelled us to survive; if we are to survive as a people in the future, it will likewise be because we were compelled by love. It's the only way.

Love you all.

Thank you to my inspirations: Maria Ross, my shining star and inspiration, my Germanic grandma who was still ridiculously Indigenous and who taught me to say "I love you" in strength, delicious food and discipline; Lyman Bullchild, who taught me to say "I love you" in spankings and basketball lessons; Gene Guardipee, who taught me to say "I love you" in weekends at his house and more spankings; Robert Reevis, my big brother, who taught me how to say "I love you" with hunting and fishing and by having difficult honest conversations; Herman Price, who taught me how to say "I love you" in Navajo breakfast burritos and smiles, and Tina Ives, who taught me to say "I love you" in sweet motherly advice and oysters. This book is also dedicated to my beautiful mom, Ger-Bear – I'm very proud of you, mama.

Thank you to all the amazing men and women who taught me how to say "I Love You" in a million different languages.

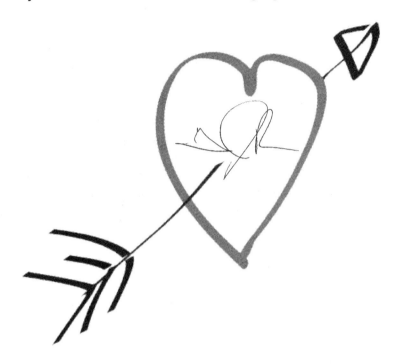

OPIUM

I was standing in the checkout line
Of the grocery store
When her scent glided by me.

I smelled her before I saw her
Dripping with perfume
Smiled
Closed my eyes
The familiar fragrance of Opium in the room
Knew it ever since I was a baby
Probably knew it in the womb
She always smelled of Opium and breath mints
And whichever flower was in bloom
Smelled like wedding flowers
Every day
What a lucky groom
Yeah
Grandma always smelled good
Even while cooking amazing food I'd soon consume
Opened my eyes
Turned around from the checkout line
See who this was making my nostrils swoon.

A little old white lady
Probably 75
Standing in the produce aisle
Squeezing watermelons and honeydews
Probably preparing a fruit salad.
She was beautiful
I went to say hi
Tell her that she reminds me of someone
And
Thank you for walking by
"You made my day."

She gave me a wink
I blushed and smiled larger
My grandma used to wink at me the same way.
She flirted with my soul
Gave my conscience butterflies

Took me back to
When I was a child sitting in church
Imagined myself going back in time
On some Marty McFly isht
Ready to make her all mine
Or at least make grandpa work a little harder
Who cares if I mess up the timeline?
Space/time continuum destroyed
As long as she cooks for me
Every night
That's just fine
Protect her from all of the ugliness in her early life
Provide for her as God designed
Cocktail dresses and pearls
Opium and a baby blue Thunderbird
Laced like Audrey Hepburn
Marilyn Monroe

I heard "It was nice talking to you
Sweetheart
But I have to go."
Opened my eyes
And I was back in the produce aisle.

Smelling Opium.

EVERYTHING THAT I NEED TO KNOW
I LEARNED IN FRONT OF THE WARBONNET

5th GRADE JAMES BOND

Everybody thought that he was the coolest kid in school.

He made it to school and to open gym every day; he never missed. Ever. And why would he? It was easier for him to get to practice than it was for anybody else at the school. Nobody ever said anything to him about it – we were in 5th grade. We were way too cool to do something like that. Still, there was always a sense of quiet admiration. Jealousy. Admiration. Worship. All the kids in our class looked at him in the same way we looked up to a senior in high school – like he was the Fonz, Rambo and my uncle who went away in the military all wrapped up in one.

But Arlen wasn't a senior. Arlen was only a fifth-grader, just like all the rest of us.

Well, he was just like us in most ways. That is, just like most fifth-graders (more or less), Arlen stood about five feet tall, wore size 9 shoes and had not received his first kiss yet. He also enjoyed watching Thundercats and Inspector Gadget, as well as WCW wrasslin' (he much preferred WCW to WWF, but it was really hard to ever watch WCW matches, except on videotape). Just like every other Indian fifth-grader, he didn't have the first traces of a mustache yet (it's important to distinguish the "Indian fifth-graders" from the "white fifth-graders" – the white kids on the rez seemed to have goatees and armpit hair by the 3rd grade). He was so much like all of us. He was a "regular" fifth-grader in almost every way, yet he differed from all of us in one very significant way.

Arlen was a fifth-grader who drove.

The crazy thing was that he didn't even seem particularly proud of the fact that he drove. In typical "little boy" fashion, Arlen's nonchalant demeanor made us admire him even more. We would whisper to each other, "It's not even a big deal to him." The lack-of-pride-in-the-coolest-thing-ever was contagious – the other boys began to act equally as nonchalant when they got a new pair of shoes or watched a new movie. That "coolness" was all inspired by Arlen.

All of us young boys wanted to be him. Arlen personified, if there was such a thing, amazing elementary school "smoothness." He was the Remington Steele of pre-teen Indian boys. Sometimes he even seemed to overdo the too-cool thing; he was so nonchalant and relaxed that it always seemed like he yawned when he talked about driving, almost like he was bored or even tired. Still, everyone knew that he wasn't really tired, that he was just too cool to even show that he might be a little bit enthusiastic about his driving. Of course, any of the other fifth graders would be doing back flips at the opportunity to drive just once. But nope, not Arlen; he was way too cool for that. He barely even talked about it; instead, he'd rather talk about the spin on his ball when he pitched in kickball.

He had kickball down to a science. Of course we all listened in rapt attention. He philosophized, "You pitch it with two hands and rub your right hand over it plum vish before you let go. That'll make it bounce just right so that they never get on."

Then he would yawn.

We listened intently, hung on each and every single word. This kid drove, for Christ's sake, so of course he knew what he was talking about. He's gotta be an expert on everything, including kickball. We sought an audience with him at recess, like he was the Pope or the Godfather. We were simply his underlings trying to get a listen to his wisdom. He was the swami on the mountaintop and we floated on his every word – all of us tried to hang out with him as much as we could.

Granted, Arlen didn't drive to school everyday, but that's didn't even matter. In fact, he didn't even drive to school most days. But none of us other fifth-graders drove on any days. Therefore, it was a big enough deal that when he did drive to school it made it seem like he drove every day. He was the driving king, even though he only drove a couple of times a week. Perception was, and is, reality – even on the rez (and oftentimes, especially on the rez).

Sometimes Arlen's mom would drop him off at school. We kind of ignored those days; on those days he was a mere mortal fifth-grader. Why did we need to pay attention to that? We could watch any one of us NOT drive any day of the week. No, the days we really paid attention were the days that he drove himself to school because, well, those were a pretty big deal. Besides, what else were we going to do with our time? We were fifth-graders. That was the big suspense before our school day: "would he get dropped off or would he drive?" On those days when his mom did drop him off, she was always very sweet and would give him a big hug before he got out of their dusty-but-beautiful brown Ford Taurus. She seemed like a great mom – I mean, she had to be an incredible mom to let him drive around the rez like she did. Every single one of us lived vicariously through Arlen – he was the kid we wanted to be. He was destined to be a reservation legend. Heck, he was already the fifth-grade James Bond; boys wanted to be him and girls wanted to be with him.

While we were sitting around on the merry-go-round one day, checking out the girls flocking around Arlen, Junior observed, "He probably already has some hair on his nuts, ennit? I mean, he doesn't have any peach fuzz on his lip yet, but I bet he's got some pretty wicked pubes, eh?"

We'd all say, "AYEZZZZZ!!! That's just rank, you! What are you, some kind of queer?? Always talking about some guy's nuts!"

But the truth is that we were all secretly wondering about Arlen's nuts too. I was his biggest fan – the short, fat, underdeveloped kid who just tagged along everyplace he went, so of course I speculated about his genitalia. But all of us did – it wasn't just me: we couldn't get the image of his probably-hairy testes out of our heads. *Maybe he was just born with bigger and hairier nuts than ours – that isn't fair! They had to be more developed; he drove, after all. Lucky hairy-nutted guy.*

Our speculation led to a reservation-wide rumor that the FordTaurus came with a "Nuts Package."[3] It was safe to say that almost all of us bought a Taurus for our first car, just in case.

FORD TAURUS

When his mom first bought the Ford Taurus, everyone could see that Arlen loved it. He acted very proud of the car and proud of his mom for working so hard to earn it. She was beautiful – the picture of what a mom should be. He loved seeing her in that gorgeous car. He'd tell us, "She earned it." So proud. That pride made him, when she dropped him off at school in it, step slowly out of the car so that everybody could get a glimpse of him from the classroom windows.

He strutted. He told me that he always looked for Elaine when he got out of the car. "Yeah, I always hoped Elaine was looking out the window when I got out. I figured that maybe if I took long enough she'd see me getting out of this awesome car."

To Arlen, sure the car was beautiful, but what it really represented was his family's improving financial status. His mom recently got off the welfare and got a job as a receptionist at the tribal college. She was working in a section of the college called the "financial aid office." It was a good job – good jobs are rare on the rez. Really, getting a regular paycheck of any kind was good money here – on the rez there's 70% unemployment, rampant alcoholism and despair, and very few permanent job prospects. There were very few job

---

[3] FYI, contrary to popular belief among the fifth-grade boys at his school Arlen did not have hair on his nuts. He happened to come from a family who carried the distinction of being one of the unhairiest families amongst the Indian families on the rez, which means that they were unhairy amongst very unhairy people already. All of his uncles only began getting a thin mustache around the age of 21 and a few thin, whispy hairs on their chins; none of them were able to ever quite "connect" their pseudo-Fu Manchu mustaches to their chin hairs. He loved to watch "Magnum PI" and since Tom Selleck was the coolest white man on the planet, this side of the Fonz, he aspired to one day have a mustache like his. He also suspected that Tom Selleck was probably a pretty hairy dude (and that the mustache was only a symptom of that hairiness), and so he wasn't against the idea of having a decent amount of hair down-below. Still, the fact was that, at that time, it just wasn't there.

prospects at all – permanent or seasonal – except for firefighting and some tourism-type jobs in the summertime. The firefighting jobs were out because Arlen's mom couldn't leave Arlen, his little sister and baby brother all alone for weeks on end while she fought fires. She was perfectly capable physically, but she prioritized her babies over that job. Plus, fighting fires was dangerous, and who was going to raise the kids if she died on the job?? She could not take that chance – their dad wasn't anyplace to be seen. Now, with this new job, she didn't have to take that risk. Life was good. In fact, life was pretty close to perfect. She wasn't making enough that they'd get accused of acting too good, but she was making enough money that they wouldn't have to worry about gas going into town or buying the kids good moonboots as winter rolled in.

It was good pay. She was a good woman. She deserved it.

Almost as important for Arlen was that his mom now had something to do during the day. It seemed like she got depressed when she wasn't working – she didn't talk that much during those times. During her layoffs, it seemed like she just stayed at home and watched All My Children and Young and the Restless and drank coffee and ate toast with jam. And smoked. And went into town to buy pull-tabs at the Warbonnet. And ended up staying at the Warbonnet till really, really late and coming home wasted. Sometimes the kids would find her passed out in the car in the morning time, in the freezing cold.

At least she'd get some sleep on those nights though, even though the sleep wasn't perfect.

Arlen wouldn't sleep at all.

He told me that he'd stay awake all hours of the night waiting for his mom. He was like an expectant father pacing around the waiting room, excited for his baby girl to arrive into the world. Or a dad waiting for his daughter's return home on prom night, hoping that his lovely daughter comes home untouched by dirty teenage boys. Or like a kid waiting for Santa Claus to come and fulfill his Christmas dreams. But instead of cookies and milk for the chubby middle-of-the-night interloper, Arlen would stay up watching Johnny

Carson (and then the rebroadcast of the local news) until the TV station went off. He'd then brew up some coffee in the coffee maker for his dear mom and stay awake and wait with a blue tin cup of warm coffee, a blanket and pillow for when she passed out cold on the couch.

Don't make any mistake about it, she wasn't a "bad" mom. Not at all. As a matter of fact, all of us boys would have loved to have her for a mom. Not just because she let Arlen drive, but because she was amazing when she wasn't drinking. She always let every one of the kids know that they were loved, and called them "Beautiful Little Lady" and "Handsome Prince" and "Incredible Little Guy" and "Baby." Despite having such a limited amount of time and energy, the kids always felt "wanted" around her – she had this incredible way of making them feel special. Any kid would be lucky to feel that! They definitely didn't have much money, but nobody on the rez really did. Still, she'd make these special little meals; she'd cook red hot dogs on the weekend and canned chili – big red chili dogs! Since the red hot dogs came in packs of three, most of the time she didn't even get one. But it didn't matter to her, as long as the kids were happy. She just cooked the hot dogs and the chili for the kids because they loved them. Mom would have some Top Ramen with an egg in it.

She was an incredible mom. When she wasn't drinking.

And it wasn't as if she drank all the time. Her drinking went hand-in-hand with her work, or lack thereof. It wasn't just her problem – that's what it seemed like with most people on the rez. When there were severe money problems, people drank. It seemed like there was more of a connection of being poor to drinking than being Indian and drinking. And she was no different – when she wasn't working, she always seemed like she was sad and she drank more. Arlen thought it was kind of weird because she never had any money when she wasn't working, but somehow she found money to drink. On the other hand, when she was working, she rarely drank even though she had the money for it.

Arlen told me that he thought it was strange. "How did she get money to drink? We don't even have money for gas."

It was obvious that he loved his mom all the time, with all of his heart. When we'd talk during sleepovers, he'd say that he felt like the Creator put them on Earth just for each other, to take care of each other. Still, Arlen also knew that he liked his mom more when she wasn't drinking, when she was working and when she wasn't sad. He thought pretty deeply for a young kid.

We'd be laying next to each other in the dark during sleepovers and he'd ask, "Do you think it's possible to love someone without liking them?"

I could tell that he wasn't sure that it was possible. I was confused by the question. Either way, when she wasn't drinking (like right now), it was very obvious that he both loved and liked her. Things were going well now, and so he was just enjoying right now.

The Ford Taurus represented "right now."

The Ford Taurus also represented his mom's new job and her current optimism. It represented a reason for her to get up every single morning and thus a reason for her not to go to the Warbonnet until the wee, cold hours of the night. It represented Arlen getting more sleep at night, a healthy amount of sleep. No more yawning and falling asleep at his desk. It represented hope that he could focus on his schoolwork and kickball and basketball, and not act like he was a worried parent. He was too young for that. He was a good student; not straight A's, but a very good and very curious student who very well might be one of the exceptional students from the rez who goes on to college and succeeds. He might be one of the few kids from the rez who makes it in the outside world and maybe comes back to make the reservation slightly better. You can always tell those kids at an early age here – by fifth grade, a lot of kids here already engage in "risky" behavior – smoking, smoking weed, sex.

Arlen didn't do any of those things – he chose to watch Karate Kid and play Galaga and Castlevania instead. Unlike many of our classmates who were beginning to experiment with hanging out with older kids and acting older than they were, Arlen loved to hang out with his little brother and sister and me when his mom was out and about. He was very fatherly, even though he never had a father around him, and was glad to be giving his younger siblings supervision. That was cool – his mom's new job represented a new opportunity for him to just be a kid. He didn't have to try to be the dad or husband or man of the house and could just be the kid listening to his mom because mom had something to be accountable to outside of her kids.

Unfortunately, things did not change nearly as much as Arlen thought they might. Her new job wasn't the magic bullet, the panacea that it seemed like it should have been. Arlen was still very much a babysitter, a kid who was required to be advanced far past his years. Yes, his mom went to work – she worked very hard, from all indications, dealing with the school administration and students. Apparently, college students weren't as carefree as fifth-graders and got really upset when they dealt with the financial aid office. When his mom got home, she seemed stressed out, tired, and ready to relax. Except she didn't want to relax at home. She would tell Arlen, "I need a smoke." Her idea of "relaxation" included some pull-tabs, and maybe a cold one. She'd drive into town to go to hang out and drive back sometimes totally blitzed.

Arlen couldn't take it anymore. He was ready to take drastic action.

He cried sometimes thinking about her being out at night. He said that he hated waiting for her all night sometimes, and wondering if she'd even make it back safely, driving drunk on the icy roads. He hated waiting. He hated the anticipation of planning how he was going to talk to his younger siblings about her being in an accident. He literally rehearsed what he was going to say to his little brother and sister – telling them, "Don't cry." and, "It'll be ok." He told me that he knew that one of these nights she just wasn't going to come home and that he would regret letting her drive. But what could he do? He was just a little kid. It's not like there was a taxi service out here on the rez. That's probably one of the many reasons why there are so many automobile deaths out here. Arlen just didn't want his mom to be one of them. He meant well.

He was tired of crying and stressing out at night and thinking about how he was going to tell his little brother and sister that she died in a car accident. He was tired of wondering where he and his little brother and sister would go when she died. He had no choice. He practiced on me because he knew it might be sort of awkward, like talking to a parent about sex. But he knew that those birds and bees discussions saved lives – he knew that if those discussions did not happen, bad stuff happened. Judging by all the young mothers in junior high school and high school, Arlen could tell that those talks did not happen nearly enough here.

That's why, like those birds and bees discussions, he knew this had to happen.

Like summer turning into fall, this conversation was inevitable and necessary even though it sucked. Still, despite the inevitability and necessity, Arlen put it off as long as he could. One very brisk night he could just tell that she was preparing for a long night of fun and flirtation – she sprayed on a lot of that Charlie Revlon perfume and put on her cowboy boots. Arlen loved the commercial for that perfume, but didn't love it when she put it on before she went out. Arlen knew that it probably meant that his mom wasn't coming home that night; the roads were probably going to ice up tonight, and she'd probably crash at a girlfriend's house. He didn't want her to stay someplace else – that always scared him, not knowing what's going on – so he decided to broach the subject with his mom squarely. He walked into the bathroom as she put her lipstick on, puckering up her lips. As his mom looked at her newly painted, puckered-up lips from different angles in the bathroom light, Arlen spoke up, just like he practiced.

"Mom, I don't want you driving around no more when you're out at the Warbonnet. It scares me."

His directness made her forget about her lipstick. Kids don't speak to their parents like that around here – they don't speak to any adults like that. "Kids are to be seen and not heard." We all heard it a million times. But Arlen's nuts, whether they were truly hairy or not, they were big. Huge. He doubled down on his boldness, "Mom, you shouldn't be driving around like that. Not when you're drunk. Not when it's icy."

His boldness made her turn away from the mirror and instead focus her attention at him. He braced for a slap. Instead, Arlen's mother's face showed surprise, but she was grinning. "You are a tough guy, baby!" She was smiling now. She looked like she got a weird rush over him taking control of the situation. She never hid the fact that she loved the idea of her son concerned about her safety. She looked proud, like she was glad that she raised a strong young man. But this was a bit different. This was stronger, bolder. She liked it when men were concerned about her – she had a very powerful and imposing father, and her so she grew very comfortable having strong men tell her what to do. Arlen was just a little guy when his maternal grandpa died, but he had a lot of her dad's characteristics. Arlen looked a lot like him, Arlen was big like him, and now he was showing his willingness to be assertive like him.

She also seemed to like it when a man, even a very young man who happened to be her son, showed genuine, loving concern. She was getting to the age where some women begin worrying about their looks fading. She was an absolutely beautiful woman; almost all of us boys at the school had a crush on her. Not just because she allowed Arlen to drive, but also because of her beautiful brown skin, long black hair and curvy body. Of course, we would never, in a million years, tell Arlen how beautiful we thought she was – that's like telling James Bond that you want to tongue-kiss his mom. Bad idea. But all of us still loved to look at her. And it was cool – she was flirtatious, innocently; she craved real male attention. The attention that she usually got was usually pretty tacky and crass. If and when they showed attention, it was usually a cat call or by making that "tsst, tsst" sound in the grocery store or probably in the bar.

The attention that her son (and us boys) gave her was different, it was sweet. And you could tell that she liked any sweet or positive attention from a male, even her own son.

She smiled at him, "I'm fine, baby." She was proud of her boy for expressing himself so openly and clearly. She didn't seem offended at all. Still, she also seemed to want to express, clearly, that she wasn't a little girl and didn't want her little boy to be worried. "You don't have to worry about anything. Your momma takes cares of herself."

Arlen narrowed his eyes a little bit, twisted his mouth over to the side as if he was pondering and nodded slowly in agreement. He was a bit more confident now after not getting slapped. He must have been doing something right. So then he went all out trying to be persuasive. Rational. "I know, Mom. But I still don't think it's safe for you to be out there on the icy roads after a hard day's work and you're so tired." He tried to project bass into his voice, but like the mythical hair on his nuts, his voice was still several years away from not being little-kid-like. "It's not your fault, Mom. You just work hard."

She grinned. She could tell that he was buttering her up. She liked it. You could tell. "Well, what do you think I should do, smart guy?"

He acted like he was just coming up with this plan on the spot, like we didn't just rehearse this conversation an hour ago. He was savvy; he didn't want it to seem like he'd been premeditating this discussion for a while. He was very aware that he was the son and she was the mom and, although he was pretty much the man of the house, he didn't want to usurp her authority.

"Hmmmmmm...y'know what, Mom? I'll drive for you. I know how – I've been paying attention watching you drive for a while. It's not a long drive. Just from the Warbonnet to home. That's all."

There. He said it. He paused for about two-and-a-half seconds and then just moved right into the next sentence because it was clear that he didn't want to give her a chance to react. He looked kind of scared of her reaction – not like he might get slapped, but like she might laugh at him like the little kid he was.

He followed the proposal with some more facts.

"Mom, brother and sister are already sleeping by the time you go to play pull tabs. They won't even know that we're gone. We'll just lock the doors and make sure that they go pee real good, drain themselves out before we leave. We just need to get back right after the Warbonnet closes so you can get some sleep for work and I can sleep before school. Can we do that – right after it closes, Mom? Please?"

He didn't look her in the eye – not like he was expecting a slap anymore, but like he wasn't sure what response to expect. Plus he still looked a little bit ashamed of talking to her so directly about such a sensitive subject.

She smiled though. She obviously appreciated his strength and resolve at such a young age. She loved for a man to take control, to pronounce what he wanted strongly. She moved her neck to the side and bent it down low, as if it to try to get low enough to catch his gaze.

"Look at me baby. Sure baby, for you...." She trailed off as she put her lipstick on, "I'll do anything for you. Of course we can do that, my little man. Thank you."

He smiled at her. He blushed a little bit – he couldn't keep the eye contact long. He was happy that he initiated this awkward conversation. He wasn't sure what she was thanking him for, but he was glad that she was willing to go along with it.

He sort of baffled his mom with BS – not to be manipulative or deceitful. He was telling the truth that he'd been paying attention to how she drove. That part was 100% true. Still, watching a person drive a car and actually driving a car are two completely different things. He had absolutely no clue how to drive.

WARBONNET

Of course Arlen loved basketball. We all did. It was kind of a law. Almost every single kid on the rez loved basketball, male and female. This place had more basketball talent, per capita, than anyplace in the country. Unfortunately, this reservation also had the highest per capita rate of amazing basketball players who didn't want to leave for higher education. Kids on the rez were infamous for that – these amazing high school careers, several state championships, ridiculous athletic ability and plenty of college interest in the sheer talent. Still, for some reason they almost always ultimately stayed at home. As a result, they almost never fully developed their talents, athletically or academically.

There was plenty of academic talent here as well.

Arlen wanted to be one of the exceptions.

He played the game of his life earlier in the day. We elementary school kids played our games in the early afternoon at the Junior High School before the junior high kids played there. Arlen scored 24 points, got a bunch of rebounds and didn't turn the ball over once. The most remarkable thing about this scoring, however, was that our entire team only scored 29 points; Arlen scored all but 5 of his team's points in the game!! Most importantly, we won; Arlen felt like a star. Some of the players from the junior high even came up to tell him "good game" and give him five. We were so jealous. Junior high kids didn't ever talk to us elementary school kids – that was against the rules. They didn't acknowledge us, really – I think one time my big brother walked me to school, but that was about the extent of it. But here they were, a group of cool junior high basketball players, and even one girl, coming up to Arlen after the game and telling him he did a great job.

You could tell he knew that he did a great job. But Arlen was so cool that he didn't even say anything other than "thanks" to the big kids. He accepted their congratulations and their high fives and just cheesed huge and put his hoodie on. He walked, fingertipping his ball back and forth between his hands, on his way to sit on the bleachers. He sat down to watch the junior high game, still fingertipping the ball back and forth. All of his teammates jockeyed for position to sit next to him while we watched the big kids play.

Arlen yawned – most of the kids sitting next to him thought, *"He's so cool. He just scored a bunch of points and has all these big kids congratulating him and he's not even excited. Plus he drives. Wow."*

Those of us who knew him best knew that Arlen was actually pretty excited. His favorite player, Gary Cross was playing. He idolized Gary – Gary worked on his game every single day, and Arlen aspired to be like that. Arlen was also actually pretty stoked that these junior high kids took notice of his game and took the time to say something nice to him about it. But Arlen was also sort of a typical Indian kid in the sense that he really didn't know how to take a compliment that well. He asked his mom that before, "What the heck am I supposed to say when someone tells me how good I am?"

She told him, "Just say thank you." And that's what he did. In the most awkward/cool way possible.

The impact from those compliments stuck with him. Ten hours after his amazing performance he told me that he was still feeling like a star. As he sat in the Warbonnet parking lot, he even had a few grown-ups come up to him and congratulate him on his game. "Hey, good game, nephew." Usually, when a grown-up called you "nephew" it was because he wanted you to run to the store for him or give him some change. Here, they were calling him "nephew" because they were proud of him. He smiled like he stole something.

And so it was an odd sight: here, in the Warbonnet parking lot, two little shaggy-pony-tailed Indian kids sitting in the front seat of a nice Taurus, smiling broadly and holding a basketball. He just couldn't turn off his smile, so he also smiled at a bunch of the other adults as they walked into the bar. Evidently, the image of a little kid smiling at you while you walk into a bar is sort of a Rorschach test for Indian people: you see what you want to see in it. Some of the grown-ups smiled back and seemed genuinely happy that this kid was happy. Some of those folks even awkwardly waved at him and a few even came and knocked on the window (or motioned for him to roll the window down) and asked him if he needed something to eat. Others weren't so cool with the sight; they seemed to think that this little boy's smile was mocking, making fun of them and possibly of their love of strong drink. Those grown-ups flipped him off and hollered at him through the closed windows. He couldn't hear what they said, but he knew that they weren't happy with his big ol' smile. Still, even their anger/shame/sadness couldn't put a damper on his amazing day.

Sitting here in front of the Warbonnet – a place where no little rez boy wanted to end up when he grew up – Arlen felt like a star. It was cool to see. He was a star. And it was easy to see that he liked being acknowledged by the grown-ups. It would be a few years before most of them knew him from basketball, but when they acknowledged him, it felt like they recognized him already.

He was a star. They just didn't know it yet.

He sat back in the front seat and smiled. He looked around. The large clock underneath the Warbonnet sign had a few light bulbs out. It alternated between the time and the temperature. Arlen could see the steam rising up off of the hot light bulbs as the sign moved between the two. 1:03. 4 degrees. "Almost there, hey." Last call at the Warbonnet was at 1:20. He rubbed his hands together and blew into them to try to keep them warm. We both noticed the steam when he blew into his hands and so he started blowing steam into the air, pretending that he was smoking. "Hayyyeeezzzz!!" It was cold; he looked like he was freezing too. He started messing with the key, turning the key over. "Let's turn on some heat, hey." The car took a few tries before it turned over; there wasn't a lot of gas in the car, still he figured that twenty minutes wasn't really that long for the car to be running. He yawned. It was a long day, a good day, but he obviously couldn't wait to bring his mom inside their trailer and go to bed.

He was very obviously ridiculously tired. He was cooler than most little kids, but he still had a hard time hiding when he was exhausted.

Arlen leaned back and looked at the clock on the radio – 1:07. Every single minute felt like another hour. "Is this thing slow?? Gawww, I wish Mom could hurry up and come out." He turned the radio up a bit and leaned back, reclining the seat as far back as it could possibly go. He adjusted his butt into the most comfortable position possible and was hoping to maybe get a couple of minutes of sleep before his mom came outside. He cuddled up to his basketball when Wham!'s Careless Whisper came on the radio – that was one of his favorite songs. He was always singing that damn song at school! Arlen, very much the romantic, was always imagining beautiful things for the women in his life: he told me that he imagined his mom marrying a wonderful gentleman who treated her exactly like he treated her. He always told his little sister that he imagined she would grow up to be the most beautiful bride to a handsome young Native man who understood how lucky he was to be with her. And, right now, under the influence of Wham! and extreme fatigue, he told me that he was imagining that he and Elaine were dancing to the song, acting out the words.

"Oh, God."

He smacked his lips and hugged the ball – eyes drooping, he pretended that the ball was Elaine. Of course he always told me that the two Wham! dudes were probably fruity, and they were probably singing the song to each other instead of to a cute girl like Elaine. "Why else would they dance like that?" Still, it didn't matter – it was a beautiful song whether they wanted to dance with a girl or boy – "None of my business," Arlen would always say. That's right: even though the song was probably written for a sweaty, hairy guy in a "Choose Life" t-shirt, when the song played in his mom's car or at their trailer, this was his and Elaine's song. And he loved it:

...Time can never mend
The careless whispers of a good friend
To the heart and mind ignorance is kind
There's no comfort in the truth, pain is that all you'll find....

He even imagined him and Elaine arguing. Yet, he told me, because they loved each other so much, they still went to the dance together and danced slow songs together. The argument was important, but being together was more important. When the saxophone solo came on, he was in a trance, thinking of him and Elaine dancing slowly, his hand on her lower back. I know for a fact that he didn't know how to dance, but he watched the nerd dance in Sixteen Candles and probably thought that he could blow Elaine's mind with his sensual moves.

ARLEN'S JOURNAL
"The Dream"

I remember that night, falling asleep in the Warbonnet parking lot. My thoughts were relaxed because I was thinking about me and beautiful Elaine dancing. Closely. My body started relaxing, and my breathing started to slow down. I took deeper breaths. No steam. It's nice and warm in here. My feet were still a little bit cold from not having the engine on — but it was warming up quickly. The dancing helped warm me up — I was really comfortable. I could still barely hear the words to the song as I soon stopped really paying attention to where I was. This car seat is pretty comfortable. It really didn't feel like I was in a car anymore. It felt like I was laying someplace, maybe in bed. My neck loosened up and relaxed, like it was rolling around, but in a comfortable way. No tension. And now, it was Elaine talking to me. Hey, it's just me and Elaine sitting in a classroom. She was sitting at a desk and I was laying in a bed right next to her. I'm glad this classroom has beds. I turned over to snuggle up closer and talk to her. Nobody was around. This is nice. "Elaine, I love talking to you. I don't feel awkward around you at all."

As I drifted off, I continued to joke with Elaine. "You're the most beautiful girl I've ever seen — even more beautiful than my mom and Jessica Rabbit!"

Of course she laughed. She jokingly said, "Jessica Rabbit?? Cripe, does that mean that there's a white girl in your top 3?"

"If she had your skin color and beautiful black hair she would be number 1!! Ayezzzzz!!!" I remember I told her that I touched the backboard in a basketball game for the first time. She looked at me admiringly, like in True Romance when Alabama tells Clarence, "You are so cool."

I felt cool. I felt incredibly cool. We talked for hours — "We should have beds in all of our classrooms. This should be mandatory. This is the best way to learn." She smiled at me again. I felt like earlier in my basketball game when it seemed like I just couldn't miss.

I opened my eyes for about three seconds as I bumped into the middle console. I smiled randomly and drooled on the vinyl seat. I could see some grown-ups walking by and looking in on me and laughing.

"Can you show me how to walk and dribble between my legs at the same time, Arlen?" Elaine was smiling her beautiful, intoxicating smile and wanting me to show her what I could do.

Of course I gladly obliged. I couldn't miss, right? Plus, even if I did miss, isn't this why the Creator created man? This was a man's job; whenever a beautiful girl asks a man to make a fool out of himself or jump through a hoop, we're supposed to do it. I got that memo — a woman like Elaine asks me to go get one of Bigfoot's butt hairs, I was absolutely going to find a way to do it. It wasn't even a question. Upon Elaine's request, I didn't waste any time at all (Pride? What's that?). I got up out of my comfortable classroom bed — and picked up the basketball (that was equally as suspiciously sitting right in the middle of the classroom). She's gonna love me after this. I began to dribble, one long stride with my left leg, flicking my right wrist to push the ball under my leg to my left hand; when my left received the rubber ball, it mirrored the right hand and flicked my wrist and pushed the ball under my right leg.

I got more comfortable and took my eyes off of the ball. I was getting into my groove. I was losing my bed legs.

I smiled and showed her what I could do for another couple of minutes, dribbling the length of the classroom and back down again, feeling more confident with each successive trip. I was the only fifth-grader who could do this without looking at the ball. Unlike my driving, this was something that I was very proud of — I felt pretty incompetent behind the wheel. On the other hand, I worked extremely hard at being good at dribbling the ball — why wouldn't I be proud?

I couldn't miss.

Just as I predicted, Elaine was impressed; I could tell. Heck, I was pretty much impressed with myself; I practically expected her to ask me if she could wipe off my sweat. She didn't. Instead, she asked me, "Can I try to dribble?"

I was honestly kind of shocked and a bit disappointed that she didn't simply fall down prostrate before me and my remarkable ball-handling abilities. Ugh. I don't want to have to correct her. That's not a very gentlemanly thing to do. Still, what could I say? "No?" That would be a butthole thing to do.

"Um, sure, of course you can...I mean, it's not like you have to ask me." I begrudgingly walked toward her with the ball. That would have been a horrible move — pass her the ball and the ball pops her in the lip. Mmmmmm...perfect lips. I briefly lost my concentration and then regained it. "Here you go."

I handed her the ball. I had to collect my composure — be the supportive man in her life. Straightening up my face, I was very prepared not to laugh at her — I had to show myself to be a gentleman, even in spite of the inevitable comedic moment. Don't laugh, PLEASE don't laugh!! To my surprise, she began dribbling competently, if unspectacularly, with her left hand. "Oh, a lefty, ennit?"

I didn't know she was a lefty.

I was taken aback; she dribbled and spoke at the same time, "No, I'm right-handed. I just think that it's important to be able to use both hands no matter what you do. I also can eat left-handed." She dribbled it in perfect rhythm, walking and dribbling. To say that I was humbled was an understatement — I was downright embarrassed that I underestimated her like this. I was also embarrassed that I couldn't even eat left-handed; I planned to start training for that tonight. Obviously it helped her ball-handling; her rhythm was so perfect, the timing between her dribbled perfect breaths.

>BANG, BANG, BANG, BANG<

Really, I was in awe watching her. Man, I really have a lot to learn. I'm just gonna go lay down on my bed again and watch. And learn. Amazing. This girl is amazing. I started to walk back over to my bed but was startled by the ball's really loud, pounding on the classroom's linoleum floor.

>BANG, BANG, BANG, BANG, BANG<.

She was practically screaming at me over her ridiculously loud dribbling, "Arlen, do you have another ball?"

I turned around just as I was about to get into my classroom bed. I looked at her sideways, wondering why she needed another ball. "Sure, I think there's one of over here in the corner. Why come? You like playing with two balls at the same time?? JAEEZZZZ!!"

She didn't even smile or break her concentration. "Can you throw it to me?" Slightly ashamed at my failed joke, I begrudgingly turned around and walked to the corner of the classroom to pick up the other ball. Sigh. I gently lobbed the ball over to Elaine and she, without stopping her dribbling with her left hand, grabbed the ball with her right hand and began dribbling it. She was now dribbling both; she was working both balls masterfully — but it seemed like they were pounding against the floor with incredible force! >BANG, BANG, BANG< Why is her dribbling so dang loud? Is she that much stronger than me? She just dribbles that ball so freakin' hard!!

>>>BANG, BANG, BANG, BANG, BANG, BANG, BANG, BANG<<<

It finally got distracting and honestly kind of scary — what is she doing to those poor basketballs??

I realized that the noise wasn't coming from Elaine. I caught the joke right about then and came to — I was sleeping! Ugh!!! I opened my eyes slowly and looked over at my little bushy-headed friend in the passenger seat; it felt like we had been sleeping forever. I saw something out of the corner of my left eye, as if something was watching me. My eyes were unfocused. I opened my eyes wide, and using the peripheral vision cultivated by no-look passes, I noticed something on my left side, out the driver's side window. I jerked away from the window, startled. I turned my head and saw a set of red eyes looking back at me in the window; I then realized that

the "banging" of the basketballs was in fact coming from the set of
hands attached to those bloodshot eyes.

>BANG BANG BANG<
>BANG BANG BANG<

"Open up, nephew!!"

WISHY

The voice woke me up! I was terrified – I could tell that Arlen was
already awake.

I could see that Arlen was terrified, too. His eyes focused, and
now he could see who was bothering him. It was a big, scary wino
who was really close to the window looking at him, steaming up the
window from the outside, hot air coming from his mouth and nose.
The big, scary wino's hands were banging on the window, trying to
get inside the car.

The wino screamed through the window, "Hey nephews, I see your
ashtray open – I know you don't know how to play any video games
because I can see that you're uncoordinated even when you sleep.
Why don't you give me that few change that's in there, hey?"

Arlen began to relax. I could see his fear soon subsided a little bit.
He rubbed his eyes and realized where he was; he was in front of
the Warbonnet. He was safe, even if annoyed. Immediately, we both
recognized who this wino was and we knew that he was harmless.
This guy wasn't dangerous, he was a guy who loved to joke around
with people and charm them out of money instead of begging them.

Arlen poked me in the ribs, "That guy. Geeeezzz...plumb rank! I bet
he needs to buy some Listerine to get drunk." Arlen rolled down the
window just a little bit to holler at the wino playfully.

"What the heck do you think you're doing, stink breath?? I was
sleeping good, you stinky guy; I don't have any money, but I wouldn't

give it to you if I did! Now just get out of here before my dad and uncle come out of the bar and roll you, you dirty old wino!"

He would never talk to any real grown-ups like this. I know he wouldn't. But unlike with his mom and other adults, Arlen felt completely justified in talking to the wino any way he wanted. "Winos ain't real adults...they're pickled people!!" Arlen and me both laughed at that image. "Pickled people."

The wino squinted his eyes and wrinkled up his nose. Arlen could see the wino's big, purplish nose up close when he pressed it up against the window – it was gross and kind of looked like a brown-colored cauliflower. We could see all the individual blood vessels and the snot coming out of his nose from the cold. Ech. The wino also wore little skinny braids; I looked at Arlen and he was kind of spacing out while looking at the wino's nasty nose and funny looking braids. That's how we knew who the wino was – because of the way that he wore his braids. See, this particular cauliflower-nosed wino tied the bottoms of his braids with bright red yarn, instead of rubber bands.

Old-style. Very distinctive. Both me and Arlen usually tucked our hair back into an unbraided ponytail (I did it because Arlen did it). He hated when his mom made him wear braids.

Arlen told me that it always seemed like the winos were the only grown Indian men who he ever saw wearing braids. Yet, for some reason, all the Indian moms always wanted their little Indian boys to wear braids. That didn't really make sense to Arlen – braids pretty much equaled "wino." "Why do I want to wear my hair wino-style? No one successful wears their hair like that," he would tell his mom. When I thought about it, it made sense. That was probably one of the reasons that so many of little Indian boys couldn't wait to cut their braids off when they were about 10, 11 years old – because they didn't want to see any bit of themselves in those stinky winos. They wanted to be the exact opposite of those stink winos – strong, active, powerful. Those winos were the epitome of "not powerful" – nobody cared about what they said or how they treated those winos.

That went double for little Indian boys who played basketball. All the little Indian boys who played basketball wanted short haircuts, like the black guys in the NBA because those black guys in the NBA were successful at something that meant a lot to them: basketball. If the best players in the NBA wore braids or guys who wore braids were generally successful at basketball/displayed excellence in something that those little Indian boys valued, (or at least something other than being a wino), those little Indian boys would probably want to wear their hair in braids, too.

If Tom Cruise or Michael Jordan or John Elway or someone who was very successful wore their hair in braids, all of us Indian boys would gladly wear our hair like that. Girls would love it! Success makes all the difference in the world; heck, if the best basketball players or the coolest guys or most successful men wore their hair in mullets with chicken poop in it, all us little boys would want to wear that – success is infectious like that.

But as of right now, the guys with braids usually didn't play basketball and generally weren't the guys who were all that successful. At least not the guys that Arlen and all of us other boys saw. The guys with braids we saw didn't play basketball and didn't have nice cars, they didn't have sexy girlfriends, they usually didn't have jobs and they really didn't even usually have their teeth. Instead, the Indian men we saw with braids drank. Lots. So we simply didn't want to wear that hairstyle no matter how badly our moms wanted us to. We didn't want to be like those guys with braids in any way, shape or fashion.

For us, braids meant bad stuff.

The big cauliflower-nosed wino tapped on the window again. The sound of the wino banging on the window made Arlen stop spacing out. He refocused his eyes (again); this particular stinky wino at his car window had little stink, skinny braids that barely touched his shoulder blades. Arlen yelled through the window, "Those little stink braids look like really long stitches." Arlen and I started laughing at that – then he called the wino "Stitches."

The wino yelled into the window again, "Come on little cousins, give me that change in your ashtray and I won't tell your mom and 'em that you were humping on your basketball and listening to snaggin' music while you were sleeping."

Arlen's face turned red, half in shame because of his "Elaine/Wham!" dream, and half in anger because this wino actually caught him dry-humping his basketball.

The purple-nosed wino continued, "Besides, little brother, that's not what you're supposed to do with a basketball – it's not made for lovin' and cuddlin' and dry-humpin' like you were doing, it's made for jammin'. That's the opposite of love – 'oooh, in your face!' Violent! I'll show you what you're supposed to do with it if you just give me that few change in your ashtray."

The clock read 1:19 – we'd barely even slept. Arlen mouthed to the bum through the window, "My dad's coming soon-you better get away, you stink wino!" He thought about it and didn't know why he was "mouthing" instead of "talking" – it wasn't as if the windows were so thick that the wino couldn't hear anything. He saw the futility of trying to mime so he stopped mouthing the words and started hollering through the window at the cauliflower-nosed man, "Besides, you houngie old fart, I'm only ten and I'd still pummel you at basketball. You wouldn't win my change from me anyways!"

Just then, Arlen's mom came out of the Warbonnet and shooed the bum away; the wino tried to flirt with her and said, "If I were in there, I'd sweep you off your barstool, sis!" His mom quickly rebuffed his advances and threw some gravel at him; the wino ran away laughing. Arlen's mom then stumbled into the backseat of the car and laid down with a smile on her face. Arlen looked back at her over the seat and got sad, but then he looked up and shook his fist at the bum as he drove away.

Arlen shouted through the window, "Sleep good, stinky!"

The old bum shot an imaginary jump shot and acted as if he made it, all net, and held his form afterwards, like he just won a game on a fade-away jumper. Then he pointed at Arlen as he drove out of the parking lot.

"Yeah right," Arlen rolled down the window and shouted out the window. "Ahhhh, you wouldn't have a chance on the court, skinny braids! Your jump shot stinks like your oosie, Stitches!"

Arlen pressed the gas for about half a second as if he wanted to peel out of the Warbonnet parking lot for emphasis. But he knew that he couldn't – that would probably be the stupidest thing this ten-year-old driver could have done. So instead, he drove about ten miles under the speed limit and also drove the backroads to their little home. There was only one Main Road, and there were always people getting pulled over there; Arlen knew to avoid it like the plague. The tribal cops were always out looking for drunk drivers, and they probably don't like little kid drivers too much either. (Although, if there was a scale, they probably like drunk drivers less than they liked ten year-old drivers. Probably.) When we finally got to his house and we dragged his mom up the stairs and into their trailer, we were both way too wired from the activity and interaction with the wino to get to sleep. They didn't have cable and the television stations had already gone off the air, so we just stayed up working on a crossword puzzle in the back of an old National Enquirer that was already started. We finally passed out at about 3:45 a.m.

We knew that we were going to be hurting tomorrow in school and at practice. I wasn't that good anyway, so it wasn't going to make much of a difference. But for him, it might affect his performance. Either way though, he was glad that his mom was safe and that he knew where she was. We still somehow managed to make it to school on time. He wanted to get there to see Elaine.

THE GROCERY STORE

Thankfully, Arlen's mom didn't go to the Warbonnet for the rest of the week. There was a very direct and obvious correlation between the two activities; whenever he didn't have to drive her around into the wee hours of the morning, Arlen played incredible basketball games.

He was a smart kid and figured out that correlation – since he didn't have to drive her around last night, he said that he was ready to play an incredible game today. To warm up his hands and get prepared for the game, he always yo-yo'd the ball as he walked to the grocery store after school to get a corndog or something to munch on before the game. We were both starving; they served that nasty square pizza today at school with all that oily cheese on it. I remember that cheese always gave him the worst farts in the world. One of our teachers once told us that a lot of Native kids couldn't eat cheese; we talked about if the government gave out commodity cheese as part of a diabolical plan to keep Indian people's stomachs upset.

Arlen would get to speculating. "Maybe that's why none of the amazing Indian basketball players go to the NBA. That's the whole purpose of commodity cheese. Hmmmmm...."

His mom was always blaming the government for something. Maybe this was just another bad thing that the government did. In either event, we couldn't afford to have his stomach hurting or farts during his game tonight; it was gonna be a tough game. He got plenty of sleep and had no excuse not to go completely Gary Cross on the other team tonight. Therefore, here we were walking to get our own food.[4] I loved watching him handle the ball; he dribbled the ball across the Main Road and into the parking lot of the grocery store. It was starting to get cold outside and I could tell that his hands were cold – dribbling the ball in the cold always hurt. But he did it anyway – that's why he was Arlen – he was different from the rest of us. "Being the best is supposed to hurt, ennit?" he would always say. When we crossed the street and got to the grocery store parking lot, we noticed the same wino from the other night at the Warbonnet, doing the running man in front two white dreadlocked ladies for some change.

That old bum could dance pretty good. Really good, actually. Maybe that's why he was making fun of Arlen dancing with the basketball – Ol' Stitches just didn't think that Arlen could dance good!!

---

[4] We sold a few comic books for some money . Comic books were a commodity and if we were lucky enough to steal a couple earlier in the day we could always get a little bit of money for some junk food.

Arlen stopped his dribbling long enough to watch the wino deftly dancing and talking to the white ladies at the same time, somehow not running out of breath. Somehow, the old, unathletic cauliflower-nosed Indian "running manned" all the way around those white ladies' Volkswagen Van, all the while giving the ladies a pretty creative sales pitch.

"Yes, ladies, this dance originated in this area. It was a ceremonial dance, and it was originally called the "Running Brave Man." But as usual, the Indians didn't get no credit. From our land to our dances, it seems like we always get burned and get our stuff stolen. But we're warriors and we know that life is like a hoop. In seven generations we'll get our land and our dances back. You'll see. MC Hammer's GREAT-great grandson will understand that Roger Rabbit was an Indian boy's pet and that's where the secret to the dance comes from."

It was pretty painfully obvious that the white ladies were buying his terrible lies. They got closer and one of them actually touched his stinky, skinny (and now sweaty) braid.

The other white lady smiled and asked him "What kind of ceremony went along with the dance?" I guess she was a little bit more suspicious of his silliness. The old bum smiled wisely, showing his pumpkin-ish smile, with three of the four bottom front teeth missing. He closed his eyes and took a deep breath as if he was in deep thought, like he was summoning up some wisdom from the ancestors, the grandfathers and grandmothers.

Arlen and I stood back and rolled our eyes. Corndogs sounded good, but this was rich.

The skinny-braided bum exhaled and began to open his mouth, "You see, my fair powdery princesses, the official, too-legit-to-quit Indian way says that you should always do the...."

Apparently Arlen had enough at that moment. Instead of simply rolling his eyes as we'd been doing, Arlen shouted to the bum at that exact moment, cutting off his words, "Hoooo, this guy!! You old stinky bum!! You better not bother me when I'm at the Warbonnet again! I'll run some Nix through your hair and then you won't have any friends left!!"

The white ladies looked over at Arlen sharply, as if he took away their opportunity for some spiritual enlightenment.

The wino tried to laugh it off and I heard him mutter something to the white ladies about how we were his "nephews" and that we were "always playing around." But Arlen didn't quit – he was calling him "Chief Thunderbird," "Little Stink Man" and "Walking Eagle" and that quickly caused the bum to break character in front of the white ladies. All of a sudden, their Indian spiritual guru had a meltdown in front of their eyes. The wino went from a smooth, calm and spiritual tone and being as charming as he could, turned toward Arlen, and quickly broke into a brisk sprint in Arlen's direction that lasted about 12 seconds before the wino doubled over in exhaustion. The wino held his side as if he had a side ache and yelled, "You lil' dusty bastard! I told you I'm gonna give you a whupping with that basketball of yours! After I whup you, I'm gonna put you over my knee and give you another whupping, you Indian rugrat!"

Arlen was smiling as he jogged backwards through the parking lot toward the road, staying out of the old wino's reaches, taunting the poor man. Arlen tormented the skinny-braided wino, "You're close enough where I can smell you, but I don't think you're close enough to grab me, skinny braids!"

The white ladies evidently weren't expecting to see the "warrior side" of the wino; seemingly understanding that the deep Indian spiritual moment was over, they opened their car doors and jumped back in their dusty Volkswagen. They threw a little change out the window onto the pavement for the wino as they drove off. The wino looked exasperated – hopeless. He screamed at Arlen and me, "You little shits! I've always dreamed, since I was just a young wino, of marrying a Birkenstock-ed white woman and driving off into the sunset in her bumper-stickered Volkwagen van." This was a little town and it seemed like no one ever drove a Volkswagen through it; everyone knew that this is a Ford and Chevy town! Now that he had his opportunity to find a white woman AND a Volkswagen van, a little punk kid messed it up. Luckily, I wasn't guilty by association for Arlen's rottenness. We could see the look in his bloodshot eyes, he wasn't about to let this little punk kid get away with this. It was obvious: he planned to teach that punk kid a lesson.

It was revenge time now.

The Main Road was unusually busy. Typically – unless it was the first or the second of the month – the traffic was always pretty light here. It could perk up from time to time late at night on the weekend when the teenagers (and the older guys who still thought they were teenagers) cruised up and down the road. This time of day, however, the traffic was usually sporadic and it was very easy to cross the Main Road. But for some reason, it was ridiculously busy, for rez standards. It was as if the pseudo-spiritual things that the wino was dancing/saying conjured up the great Thunderbird from the sky and he caused traffic to make crossing the road impossible. Arlen was trying to get far away from the wino, but he couldn't seem to get across! He had to get across – he pissed off this cauliflower-nosed Indian man, and now he was coming to get him. Quickly – the wino was working his way through side aches and being out of breath and kept on pushing through. Like Jason or Michael Myers. Arlen looked back at the bum quickly running across the parking lot – and looked out across the busy Main Road, and just could not find an opening to cross the road. Arlen looked like he was in a real life game of Frogger, and the snake was quickly approaching – except this snake's name was Stitches. The wino ran through his side ache and pushed his braids out of his face. Arlen made a couple of fakes as if he was just going to run into traffic, but then wisely came back to the side of the road every time. The wino caught up to him and grabbed him by the ear.

"You little shit, get over here!" The wino was stronger than he looked! He had Arlen by the ear and the scruff of the neck and pulled him back toward the grocery store. I could tell that Arlen wanted to cry and we were both wondering what the wino had in store for him. He was scared, and trying really hard not to cry. I stuck close in case something really bad was going to happen.

"Ow, c'mon, I was just joking! Slow down! Take it easy! Ouch... please let go...stop."

No one around the grocery store even gave the scene a second look. For one thing, it was starting to get twilight and maybe people didn't really see what was going on. But aside from that, it really wasn't that unusual to see an uncle or grandpa disciplining their nephews/grandsons through shaming and/or mild physical violence – that's what happened here and that was an uncle's job. And so Arlen kept walking and leaning wherever the bum wanted him to go; he was leaning headfirst slightly and toward the left, because the wino pulled him with his right hand holding Arlen's left ear.

Arlen was holding back the tears now – he had that hard-breathing thing going on. I wasn't crying, but I was nervous that I was going to have to find a bottle to break or something. I thought maybe Arlen was going to get killed or raped or chopped up. I heard about grown-ups kidnapping little kids, and I was pretty sure that's exactly what was happening. The two of them walked past the front entrance and were now going around the corner toward the back of the store. Arlen wasn't talking so tough or funny anymore; he was definitely toning down the insults and funny comments – "Look man, I don't even know your name. Ouch, that hurts. What's your name?"

"My name is Wishy but you really don't care, do you? You don't care about who I – I'm just a wino to you, ennit? Now you're just scared, you little shit. Don't try to talk your way out of this. I told you that I was going to teach you a lesson, and I'm going to teach you a lesson. I'm going to do what someone should have done to you years ago, you little punk: I'm gonna teach you some respect!"

Wishy pulled him to the back of the store – Arlen's ear was all red from the pinching and the cold. When Wishy let go, Arlen rubbed his ear gently, looking like he was trying to console it or trying to warm it up. I got my ears pierced when I was eight years old because my mom wanted me to be a grass dancer; she numbed my ears by putting clothes pins on them. The clothes pins didn't really make the pain any less, it just hurt so bad that the piercing kind of just blended in.

That's what his ear looked like now. I rubbed my ears because just the sight hurt me.

They turned the corner and got way ahead of me. Arlen somehow looked lost only a few hundred feet from the front of the grocery store, a place where he always felt at home. He was at this store pretty much every day – asking grown-ups for change, stealing candy, playing video games, etc. Oddly, Arlen never went to the back of the grocery store. None of us ever came here before – why would we? There was just a bunch of big dumpsters and pallets for hauling in groceries. There was no one else in back. Not a soul, except for a few rez dogs. It was hard to believe that this was the same building. It looked completely different from the store we were so familiar with. This was lonely. And scary. There were seemingly hundreds of people in front of the store, but there was only Wishy and Arlen and me here.

I didn't want to be here.

As they arrived at the back of the store, I saw Wishy slap Arlen on the ear. "Ow, piss! Don't do that man! Look, I was just joking around, Wishy. I didn't mean anything by it." Arlen had tears in his eyes, and clutched his basketball tightly.

"Now give me that ball, you little punk." Wishy began to take off his jacket and toque. I thought that Wishy might be undressing to do some raping. I began looking around for a bottle or a crowbar.

Arlen looked confused, like he was scared about what he said – he turned white with fear. "Huh?"

"Give me the ball."

"I'm not giving you any balls, you old queer bum."

"Shut up you little punk, I'm not gay. I don't want your little underdeveloped balls. I want your basketball! You don't know what you're doing with it. Hurry! I hope I can still catch those sexy white ladies at the gas station."

Arlen exhaled in relief. By that time, I caught up to them and was out of breath. But I heard him say that he didn't want Arlen's balls, so I exhaled in relief, too (and almost threw up). We were still definitely nervous about what might happen, but it sounded like one of the worst possible scenarios was off the table. That was a relief. Arlen stopped clutching the basketball so tightly and humbly handed it over to Wishy.

I stood on the wall and vomited.

"Now, you said that I don't know what to do with it. I'm going to show you something. Take this ball from me, you little queer." Wishy backed up about 15 feet from the wall of the grocery store, "Stop me from getting to the wall. I'm going to dribble to the wall and you're not going to do anything to stop me. But I want you to try. Punk."

Arlen looked shocked, like he couldn't believe this stinky old bum was going to try to beat him at basketball. I was shocked, too – Arlen was the best at basketball. *Why does the bum want to embarrass himself even more?* The bum began to dribble. Between his legs, slowly, strongly, confidently; he was not slapping the ball or letting the ball control where his hands went. No, he controlled the ball. It was pretty obvious that the bum knew what he was doing – I could see it from the first ten seconds he dribbled it. The ball was part of his hand. "HURRY!!" Wishy was getting impatient, and I was (and I think Arlen was, too) simply shocked that this wino with tiny braids and a cauliflower nose could handle the ball like he did.

"Ok. My defense is pretty good though." Arlen crouched down into a textbook defensive position – back perfectly straight, knees bent as if he were sitting down, legs shoulder width apart. He got between the bum and wall as Wishy faced him directly, barely touching Wishy's hip with his right hand. They were mirror images, Arlen's left hand playing defense on Wishy's right hand. Wishy put his right foot forward and made a quick dribble toward the right with his right hand, protecting the ball with his left hand; Arlen slid his left foot to the left about 6 inches to cut off Wishy's move. Wishy then quickly crossed over to his left, below Arlen's reach, and took a quick jab step with his left foot. Arlen was playing great defense, anticipating that move, and slid slightly backwards, cutting off Wishy's move to the left. However, as if Wishy already knew that Arlen was going to anticipate Wishy's move back to the left, Wishy quickly wrapped the ball around his back with his left hand dribbling it over to the right hand, leaving Arlen moving to his right while Wishy had a clear path to the wall on his own right side. Now the old, smelly bum who couldn't run ten feet without getting a side ache looked cat quick and left the youthful, well-conditioned kid stumbling over his own feet.

Wishy slammed the ball against the wall.

"Punk. I hope you learned your lesson. You're good against other people just like you – against little blank-shooting shits who think they're a lot better than they really are. You're good against other scrubs. But you're no good against people who actually understand how to play. You need to be good against everybody. Stinky old bums included."

Arlen and me just watched as Wishy casually put his jacket and toque back on. Wishy was sweating and breathing hard and Arlen was not. But it didn't matter much – despite Arlen's superior conditioning, he didn't even deserve to be on the same court as Wishy. That was clear. Wishy couldn't run ten feet, but he was a much better basketball player than Arlen.

Wishy grabbed his backpack and walked toward the gas station to find his future wife, blonde hair and in Birkenstocks, in her Volkswagen bus. He never turned around.

Arlen picked up his ball from the wall. He stared at it a few minutes – neither one of us could believe that Wishy was that quick, could handle the ball that well. I didn't have to say anything to him – he already knew. He just got whupped by a stinky old bum. Badly. He looked up at the sun – the sun was almost gone. We knew what that meant, so we ran off toward our game. Our team was scheduled to begin warming up in about 20 minutes.

We made it in time – him in time to play, and me in time to sit on the bench and cheer him on.

It was a great game. Arlen scored 27 points and played the best defense that I'd ever seen him play in his whole life – he shut down the point guard, #21, a tiny kid with goggles who wore braces on his teeth. Arlen's tendency before would be to relax on defense and focus on offense against a funny looking kid like #21. But seeing as a bum just made him look like the worst basketball player on the rez, he worked harder than I ever saw him work in his life! If a bum could whoop him, it was pretty obvious that he couldn't take anyone lightly. Wishy showed him – in only about 5 minutes of playing behind the grocery store – that you cannot underestimate anybody.

It was a thing of beauty.

Arlen didn't underestimate the little goggled, brace-faced kid; he dominated him, like he never dominated before. Afterwards, the junior high school coach asked him if he would practice with them. Arlen asked his fifth-grade team coach, who said, "Sure. Just make that you're not even more tired when you come to our practice."

MENTOR

Arlen always told me how much he hated his mom drinking. He always told me how much he hated drunks and hollering, Wild Irish Rose Whiskey, Thunderbird, fights outside the Warbonnet and his mom using him as an excuse for why men could not come home with her. He hated being tired in the morning, and also hated being tired at night. He hated being exhausted during basketball practice – he always said that he could play better if given the chance, and he also knew that he could get even better grades if given the chance. If he didn't have to drive Mom around all night. Her drinking was getting more frequent. It stayed steady in fifth and sixth grade, but around the time that we went into seventh grade and his little brother and sister began going to school full-time, it got much worse.

Arlen was a mama's boy. That's why he hated it – seeing his mom falling apart in front of his eyes. She wasn't Superwoman to him anymore. She wasn't perfect anymore. Arlen was a smart guy, but he knew that nobody was perfect. Still, his mom was a goddess to all of us when we were little kids. Powerful. Smart. Beautiful. She was beautiful when she wasn't drinking; heck, she was even beautiful when she was drinking. But she changed – she prayed more when she was drinking. She cried more when she was drinking. We would sometimes hear her praying and crying at the same time. She prayed that her kids would never start drinking. She prayed that her kids would find love and a husband or wife who respected them and didn't hit them.

She prayed so beautifully. Nobody prayed like that in my family. She prayed passionately. Painfully. Despite how painful it was to hear her pray like this, both Arlen and me loved the way it sounded when she prayed. So he told me that we were going to start praying like that, for our friends and family in the same desperate and beautiful manner. Elaine. My family. My big sister. We prayed for all of them every night.

One time, after we got back from the bar, we took ourselves to sleep. I thought his mom would immediately fall asleep too – she was usually passed out by the time we got to their house. We typically had to carry her in. This time, Arlen wasn't sure whether she never went to sleep or whether she woke up in the middle of the night. Either way, Arlen woke from hearing her crying. He shook me, "Do you hear that?" We both got scared and thought that maybe his mom was having a fight with someone so we put our ears against the wall so we could hear better.

She was still very drunk. Clearly. But we could hear her praying between drunken sobs, "A'pistotooki, Creator, please...I love my kids so much...y'know I want some company, God, but I don't want to bring strange men around my kids...I don't want my kids to ever see a man hitting me, Lord...I don't want them to go through any of that shit – that's why I'm alone, God. They deserve better than that. I don't know if I any deserve better than that, but they do. If I don't deserve better, let me suffer the loneliness and sadness for my kids... please help them find true love and forever love so they won't ever be tempted to start boozing...please God...I don't want them to drink, please let my babies find good partners...God, I don't want to drink anymore. I don't want my brave little boy to have to drive me around. I don't want him to think that he has to take care of me." Neither of us were quite sure how those things went together – drinking, being hit by someone they loved, and being heartbroken. Still, it seemed like they went really closely together. Arlen would usually be crying by the time she trailed off and passed out.

Arlen was my hero. When your hero cries, you cry, too. I cried a lot.

He went in her room and took the beer from beside her bed. He spilled the beer down the sink, covered her up with a blanket and wiped the smeared makeup from her face.

It broke my heart – I hated this. Arlen hated it too. I don't know which he hated worse, her drinking or knowing that she carried around a broken and lonely heart for her kids.

Still, as much as he hated seeing all those things – the fights, his mom falling apart, the drunks, the liquor bottles – strangely, he seemed to love going to the Warbonnet. We knew that every single time that he went to the Warbonnet late at night, he got to work with Wishy. Wishy made him better at basketball – in the past year and a half that he'd been working out with Wishy late at night, he'd gotten so much better. And he loved getting better at basketball. Wishy also taught him about respecting everybody, that you cannot judge a book by its cover.

Wishy made Arlen a better person.

Tonight, we brought his baby brother and sister with us to the Warbonnet – they were out of firewood and it was too cold to leave them at home with no fire. The heat was blasting. The little ones were sleeping in the backseat of the car. His little sister was six now, in first grade, and a little too independent for her age. She was already used to getting herself up when they arrived home around two o'clock in the morning. She already knew that Arlen's hands would be too busy dragging their mom into the trailer and carrying baby brother. There was no way that he would be able to bring her in at the same time. So she forced herself to wake up when she heard the "door is ajar" sound. Then she forced herself to get up again and get dressed at seven o'clock because Arlen was trying to get Mom up at that time so that she could get to work and get baby brother ready for kindergarten.

He already had his hands full. She was too aware of that fact.

Arlen looked at the clock radio – it read 11:37. He glanced back at the little ones sleeping in the back. The kids looked like angels, snoring that little baby snore. He turned back and faced the front of the bar, folded his hands behind his head and reclined the front seat. Just as he relaxed, a familiar face tapped on the window. A big, cauliflower nose. "It's about time," Arlen muttered. Arlen smiled and opened the door and we all felt the incredibly cold blast of air hit us. This was going to hurt his hands every single time the basketball hit them – it was cold to me, and I wasn't even going outside. Still, he grabbed his basketball and stepped out the door and got ready to play.

He knew that I had his baby sister and brother and that they were ok; that was my excuse for staying in the car. Plus, we were fixtures by now; everybody at the Warbonnet knew us and nobody would ever mess with any of the kids.

The cold breeze blew right through me – I knew that Arlen and Wishy had to be freezing. The wind here had a way of penetrating to your soul – there were no clothes that were sufficient. My grandma used to say that the cold wind was stronger near the bars because the spirits were crying for help. They cried much louder near the bars. He should have worn sweats under his jeans.

As usual, Wishy and Arlen walked over toward the big industrial, steel garbage can at the back of the unpaved parking lot. It was out of the way of incoming traffic, but in a spot where he could easily see me and his little sister and brother sleeping. The garbage can was Wishy and Arlen's basket – it was crude, but perfect for teaching someone to play defense. You just had to literally stop the person from getting to the garbage can by any means necessary. Usually Arlen had to stop Wishy from getting to the basket and dunking on him.

Tonight was different, though. I rolled down the window, in spite of the cold, because I liked to hear Wishy trash-talking Arlen. I heard Wishy say to Arlen, "Tonight, you're on offense. I want you to focus on getting your shoulder down low and past me. Once your shoulder is past me, you should be gone with the wind, little bro. It's almost impossible to recover once someone has their shoulder past you – they have to go across your body. You have to make sure and get really low on both sides. You gotta be just as strong to both sides, so we're going to go 100 times to each side."

Wishy gave Arlen the ball. Arlen crouched down in a "triple threat position" to the right side, right foot forward, facing Wishy. He drove to the right side and Wishy slid by Arlen's right side subtly, stepped in front of Arlen and stopped Arlen cold in his tracks. Arlen ran right into Wishy. Wishy was calm, professorial, like a braided Mr. Miyagi. "See, the way I stopped you cold? You have to beat them to the spot." They did this over and over, and Arlen never did get past Wishy. Arlen's hands were numb from being exposed to the cold, his legs hurt from crouching down – still he understood that with every single failure here in the Warbonnet parking lot, he was getting better. Arlen was so far ahead of his competition; nobody his age was going to play defense like this old drunk here. The pain in his hands and legs was going to pay for his college education. He just needed to keep listening to Wishy and keep on working hard.

He kept working hard. Warbonnet lessons, practice, running.

In his seventh-grade season, Wishy began to go to his games. Wishy would never sit down – he'd just stand in the entrance to the gym where no one could see him. You could tell Arlen was happy to show Wishy that his lessons weren't in vain. He applied the painful lessons and was, by far, the best seventh-grade player in the county, maybe even the state. Offensively, defensively, it didn't matter – Arlen was prepared for games in a way that the area had never seen a seventh-grader be prepared.

Our coach liked to take credit for his improvements. Even though he knew that Arlen worked with Wishy on certain specific skills, the coach's pride wouldn't allow him to think that an old wino's influence was infinitely more important than his.

Between games at their Warbonnet sessions, Wishy would sometimes pause and tell Arlen about how he got so good. One particular warm summer night a few weeks before we began eighth grade, they actually did more talking than playing. They finished playing a little bit earlier than usual. Wishy went to go drink some water from a mayonnaise jar beside the car. Afterwards, he didn't grab the ball again; instead, he just leaned against the car in the parking lot, while Arlen walked over to the car and sat in the driver's seat with his legs sticking out and the door open. I took my usual spot in the passenger seat and pretended that I didn't hear what they were talking about.

They were both sweating and guzzling large amounts of water. Wishy looked over at Arlen kind of angrily, like he had something really important to say to him. Then he put the mayonnaise jar down and began to talk to him. Aggressively. Urgently.

"I can tell that you feel real good about yourself. I can see it. I mean, you should, but I can tell." Wishy paused.

Arlen looked a little bit nervous sitting down, like he felt like he should be standing up. This was different than any way that I'd ever seen them communicate before. This looked like Wishy was really angry at him. I was nervous, and he wasn't even talking to me. "Yeah, I was just like you, I had the same walk that you have. I was different. I came from a family that liked to drink, too, just like yours. My mom liked to be at the bar, too. She was like your mom – she was a really good mom. But she had an addiction, a sickness. She liked the bar, but she always made sure we had clothes and food – my dad sure didn't do that. But she liked the bar. That's how she dealt with pain and pressure. Hell, that's even how she dealt with happiness and celebration. Either way, it seemed like there was always an excuse to drink. My dad was just plain a drunk. He wasn't a good dad. He wasn't like mom at all."

Arlen shook his head in agreement. He knew all about the dads. Him and I would talk about why dads were more inclined to be like that. We all knew that his mom wasn't an angel – she was here at the Warbonnet way too much. But at least she was here. His dad was never here. He and his mom both said that they had no clue where his dad was. His mom had to deal with the stress for both her and his dad because his dad didn't have to deal with any of it.

Realistically, life had to be tough here on the rez for grown-up Indian men. They are told that in order to be a "real man" or a "real dad" they have to be able to financially take care of the family. Yet, there are hardly any jobs here, and the jobs that are here ain't that good; the odds are stacked against them. As a result of how bad the economy is here, even the best-intentioned man had a difficult time being a "real man" according to those shallow criteria. That was tough. That probably affects the way that a man looks at himself and values himself. He and I talked about that. But still, Arlen told me, "I know that it's not easy to take care of your family around here. It probably makes it difficult to feel like you're doing your job as a dad or a husband. But...at least he could try. If he tried and was unsuccessful, at least he was trying...and we'd know that he thought it was worth his effort." That was the thing about his mom that he loved – she always tried. All the time, she was trying to do something better for them, even if it wasn't perfect. That's why all of us boys thought that Arlen was so lucky; he and his little brother and sister saw their mom every day. A lot of us didn't see either. She wasn't a dad, but she tried hard to play both roles, so it was like they saw their dad everyday.

Arlen replied to Wishy. "Yeah, I wish my dad was around more."

Wishy looked at Arlen, and he didn't seem angry anymore. He looked at him real sadly. Like he pitied him. "Arlen, I know you look up to me. And I know we're friends and you like the way that I play basketball. But don't be like me, little nephew. I remember that I used to promise that would never be me – inside the bars, drinking. So I did the opposite. I always worked out, I was always doing push-ups, and I was always playing basketball. By the time I got to high school, every college in the region wanted me to play for them – they didn't even recruit Indian ballplayers back then at all, but they wanted me. But y'know, little brother, history repeats itself if you're not careful. We do exactly the same thing as our parents if we don't pay really close attention. It's in our genetics, bro. I started to think that I was that special my junior year in high school. I mean, shit, why not? They had parades for me, they gave me an honoring ceremony and a headdress at 16 years old. Of course I'm special, right? I started to think that I could sneak a drink here and there and...well, damn, here I am little bro."

Wishy dribbled the ball a few times, then put the ball down and wasn't even looking at Arlen anymore, although it was very clear that he was still talking to him. He continued, "You know, I'm not going to tell you not to drink, little brother. Here I am, a freakin' wino; I can't tell you the last time I went a day without drinking Thunderbird. How in the hell can I tell you not to drink? That would be stupid. I may be a drunk, but I'm not stupid. I know I look like an old ass man, but I'm not even that old bro. I'm not even forty years old yet – I'll be forty in the spring. I know that sounds old to you now, but you'll soon realize that forty is way too young to be looking like I do. I look terrible. I used to be a handsome young man with the whole world in front of me and a jump shot that couldn't miss. Just like you. And that's why I can't tell you anything. But I will ask you something though...the only thing that I'll ask of you is this, bro...you are very special, you are a very nice kid. You have so much love in your heart and you take care of your mom and your little sister and brother. You love your mom – you should love your mom. She's an angel. She gave birth to you and she's still giving birth to you every single day. She keeps giving you life every single day – a mom's work never stops. You keep loving her like you're loving her – don't get discouraged, little man. That alcohol will make you not love her the same. Trust me. I ask you to trust me when I tell you that you cannot love all those people that you love in the same amazing way once you start drinking. Drinking takes away from your love – it makes it dirty. It'll make your love of basketball dirty because you won't be able to play basketball as good as you do now. It'll make your love for your mom and sister and brother feel dirty and not right because you won't be able to take care of them the same way. You'll feel helpless, like I do, trying to love the people you love but not being able to do anything to help them. You're special little brother, but you're not that special. Just like it did to me, it'll make it so that you can't love right."

By this time, Wishy was crying. Arlen started crying, too. It was really, really hard to see a grown man crying. Almost any grown man would probably rather jump off a cliff than let another man see him cry. Arlen was seeing something that he wasn't supposed to see. But Wishy was allowing us to see it anyway. It was a gift. Wishy went on, "I'm a wino. I make a lot of bad decisions and do a lot of stupid stuff. I'm not stupid, but I do stupid stuff. I drink way too much. I'm ashamed to see my family and so I haven't even seen them in over two years. Then I stopped making decisions – pretty soon, what used to be a bad decision wasn't a decision anymore. Pretty soon, I didn't make the decision to drink anymore – that's just what I did. I drank. I'm a drunk. And pretty soon you're just drinking to go through the motions and basketball and your mom stop being important. Or at least it stops being as important as drinking. Please trust me, little bro – you won't love the same."

I didn't really understand what he was saying – I don't think Arlen did either. We were little kids. How could we understand the depth of Wishy's words? It didn't matter though, because we understood that Wishy really, really meant it and it must be really, really important. Wishy never had one of these kinds of conversations with him before. They always just talked about basketball. If Wishy chose to talk to Arlen about something other than basketball, he must have thought that it was really, really important. Because of that, Arlen was pretty much willing to tell Wishy whatever he wanted to hear to let him know that he would never stop loving basketball. He told Wishy that his lessons weren't in vain. He assured him, "I promise that I will never drink, Wishy. I understand what you're saying. I promise. Thank you."

WINTER

The winter of our eighth-grade year, Arlen grew six inches; he went from 5'8" to 6'2". All of a sudden, he could dunk. Easily. That winter, around Halloween, we also stopped seeing Wishy in the Warbonnet parking lot. We didn't see him at the grocery store begging for change either. That wasn't too uncommon – many of the winos disappeared during the wintertime to find a much warmer place. This was a particularly cold winter – extremely bitter, with lots of snowfall – so we knew that Wishy was probably at a relative's house staying warm. There were no lessons that winter, although it didn't matter much – Arlen was so incredibly far ahead of every other eighth-grader in his league that college recruiters already showed up at his games from time to time. He was the best product out of this county since Gary Cross. Plus, he couldn't play all that much in the Warbonnet parking lot anyway; the record amount of snowfall wouldn't allow it.

He still hated driving in all the snow. But he had to make sure that his mom got home safely. It seemed like he was driving her home more than ever. The only good part about it was that the owner of the Warbonnet would let us come into the lobby part, where no alcohol was served, and stay warm and sleep until his mom got done for the night.

He told me that he dreamed about going to college and marrying beautiful Elaine. He told me that he also dreamed about the promise that he made to Wishy.

I knew that he took what Wishy told him to heart; we both promised that we would never, ever drink in our lives. Arlen promised himself that he would set a better example for his little brother and sister than the one that his family set for him. He wanted the cycle of self-medicating through alcohol to end with him; he started to take his brother and sister with him to his basketball practices. I usually watched them while they dribbled around and Arlen practiced. Arlen also learned how to cook so that they could taste how much he loved them – he wanted his love for them to always be beautiful (and tasty). Also, he tried to make sure that they did not have any excuses in the morning – he didn't want them not to perform well because they were tired, hungry or stressed out.

Like he was when he was a little kid.

That season, he averaged a triple double. More importantly, none of the players he guarded scored more than fifteen points all season. He was the defensive stopper on the team and the guy who the other team simply could not stop. Plus, he got straight A's – colleges were already salivating at the opportunity to recruit this long-haired Indian kid. They knew that he was somehow different from many of the other Indian basketball players – he didn't seem to make excuses for anything. There was so much talent on the rez and those recruiters looked forward to the opportunity to nab them. But they also always knew that there would be problems with grades and adapting. Arlen was different. He welcomed responsibility and challenge. He didn't underestimate anybody or anything – he played hard every single play of every single game.

After the season, he would drag me to the gym to begin lifting weights and start getting stronger for the more physical high school game. He told me that he couldn't wait for springtime – he knew that he was going to improve so much this summer, and that it would feel amazing to run in the sun. He told me what he needed to do, "Get bigger, faster, stronger – don't underestimate anybody, Those guys are in the gym working right now, getting better. Work harder than them. No excuses!"

I told him, "Geez man, you sound like Gunny Highway."

And he was that committed. The weather was finally warming up, and he got excited because he could see some of the hard-packed ice from the rough winter was melting.

One day, while we were jogging to the community pool where the weight room was, he was talking about the warm summertime sun. He said that he'd been daydreaming about the sun a lot lately, and couldn't wait to exercise in it. He said that in his daydream, he was running with no shirt on in the brush, dodging prairie dog holes and badger holes. He had big chest muscles in his daydream – Elaine liked to watch him run by her house. I was struggling to keep up, my eyes closed in agony – I hated running. Then all of a sudden, I hear a loud "Ouch!" I thought it was me – Arlen never got hurt.

I looked over and Arlen was laying on the ground in pain. He was pointing to a big chunk of ice on the side of the road. He stubbed his toe. "That freaking thing hurt! Freakin'...thing!!" I was catching my breath and walked over; we both looked a bit closer and saw something in the melting ice. "Bigfoot??" Our families were pretty superstitious, and so Bigfoot was always a reasonable possibility. We definitely believed in Bigfoot. "Ahhh, that's not Bigfoot," Arlen said, although I could tell that he still thought it was a possibility. But we knew it probably wasn't.

Maybe it was a coyote or a wolf or something.

Heck, we could be famous even before Arlen made it to the NBA. We'd at least be famous on the rez. Taking a closer look, it didn't look quite as big as we initially thought it was – Sasquatch is supposed to be huge. "No Arlen, that thing isn't Sasquatch... he'd be at least twice that size. What the frigg??" Sometimes a dog would get caught in a snowstorm – maybe it got run over by a car or was injured by a badger in a fight. When snowstorms came around sometimes the dog's wounds would not allow him to make it to anyplace warm. When that happened the dog would have no choice but just stay there and try to stay warm until the cold front passed. Usually what happened though was that the dog just froze there and stayed under a thick sheet of ice until the springtime.

Maybe that happened here.

It definitely looked like some big old dog or deer in a block of ice under a snow drift. We really couldn't tell though because the ice was really thick and was colored that nasty, dirty, slushy color that snow turns in the spring. Either way, we knew that there was a small possibility that it could still be Bigfoot, so we wanted to make sure that we got credit for it just in case. We ran to the indoor pool and told the front desk person that there might be some animal frozen outside and that it was really big. Arlen jokingly added, "It looks like Bigfoot," just in case it was. Then we went about our workout and went home.

A few days later on, we found out that it was a person inside of that block of ice, and that the person had been frozen in there for several months. From what the people at the community pool were saying, the person passed out in the snow and just never woke up. It seemed like that happened to a few people every year.

A few nights later, we found out that person in the ice was Wishy.

It was a warm springtime evening so Arlen was dribbling the basketball outside of the Warbonnet. One of the other winos who frequented the parking lot told Arlen that it was Wishy because he recognized him from the two of them playing ball together. That other wino also told Arlen that Wishy watched every single one of Arlen's games from the sixth grade on, which Arlen never knew.

When we found out about his death, Arlen didn't cry. Wishy wasn't perfect. He was important to Arlen, and I guess me too, but he wasn't perfect. Arlen told the wino "thank you" and went to sit in the car and turn up the music. "Careless Whisper" was on again. I didn't ask him what he was thinking about, but I could tell that he was holding back tears like that day behind the grocery store. I could tell he was thinking about Wishy.

PROMISE

We both kept our promises to Wishy – Arlen never underestimated an opponent again. Never. Parents sometime yelled at him during his games because he played just as hard when his team was winning by 40 as when the score was tied. Still, he made it very clear that he was never going to give less than all of his effort – win, lose or draw. Also, like me, he never drank alcohol; he told me that he understood, finally, what Wishy meant by "not being able to love the same." Wishy loved Arlen. Arlen knew that – anybody who was ever around them knew that. But because Wishy was embarrassed to come inside at the games, he never showed his face to let him know how much he supported him. It affected his love for Arlen.

Wishy was right.

Finally, Arlen told me that he wasn't ever going to focus on whose hair was long or short – Michael Jordan or Tom Cruise or whomever. He was going to be his own man, proud of his hair, proud of himself. He told me that he was going to keep his hair long – as long as he played, he would have long, strong braids that he tied up with red yarn at the bottom in honor of Wishy. As fate would have it, "as long as he played" ended up being a very long time. He ended up having a very successful high school career – a straight A student as well – and got the opportunity to play basketball in college.

He did well in college – I was the team's manager. I saw his solid statistics every single game. He wasn't an All-American, but he averaged double-figures and was known as a very good defender. The reason that he played so good on defense was because of Wishy's lessons. He worked hard every single day and made sure that he was always prepared. If some out-of-shape old bum could beat him, he knew that he couldn't take anyone lightly.

And he didn't. As a result of his work ethic in the classroom and on the basketball court, his college experience was pretty amazing.

Throughout that entire amazing college career, Arlen kept his word. Sometimes he got teased about the braids – some of the opposing schools had pretty primitive cheering sections and they called Arlen "Chief" or did the weird Atlanta Brave "War Whoop" thing. Arlen didn't seem to care at all – if that was the worst thing that he had to worry about in life, he was doing alright. It didn't seem to make him want to cut his braids at all; his goal was to give the little kids back home someone to look up to who wore braids. We both remembered what it was like to not have anyone with long hair we could look up to. He worked to change that. After all, he was someone who played basketball very well and who was somewhat successful. And he had braids – Arlen was doing his best to show that successful guys can have braids too.

He also always made sure that those younger boys saw beautiful Elaine with him – he was very proud to show them that, yes, guys with braids can get the beautiful girls, too. *Elaine is amazing and she loves bushy braids!* Arlen helped put on basketball camps back on the rez during the summertime for the young kids – and he began to notice more of the young boys wearing braids. That made him happy. A couple of them even had red yarn tied at the bottom, too.

As for his braids themselves, Arlen wasn't that good at braiding his own hair. Big fingers. In fact, that's how he first got Elaine to hang out with him – he asked her to braid his hair. They were inseparable after that. In fact, Elaine braided his hair for him before every home game. We all went to college together and they got engaged in the middle of our junior year.

Finally, right before his "Senior Night," the last home game of our senior season in college, Arlen cut off his braids and silently gave thanks for the wino who taught him to truly play basketball and to not sacrifice his love for anything. It was a three-person ceremony – Elaine, Arlen and me. Everyone was shocked when he came to his last game with a crew-cut. Still, Arlen seemed to be very comfortable with his decision (and his haircut) and knew that he'd kept his promises.

It was customary for parents to attend Senior Night – Arlen's mom made it. He was so proud of her; she came out onto the floor and he handed her a red rose. She looked powerful. Smart. Beautiful.

And recovering. She hadn't had a drink in two years. Her handsome little boy, Arlen's little brother, got into her stash one night; strangely, that shook up her world. She never even saw that as a remote possibility because Arlen was an angel. Arlen was incredibly strong, incredibly mature – most kids aren't like that. Arlen's little sister – one year older than their baby brother – also was a woman at an early age and took care of their mother. Like Arlen, she never drank either. They both gave their mother the impression that her drinking didn't affect them.

But it did affect them. One night when Arlen's little brother was 15 years old he got alcohol poisoning when he and a friend found his mom's stash of Laird's Vodka and Miller Light. He could've died. All the nights that she could've died didn't affect their mom – the one time that her baby could've died, however, changed her life.

That was the wake-up call she needed. "Never again," she told her youngest son and daughter. "You'll never see mommy drink again."

And they never did.

Arlen's little sister had to drive for their mom when she turned twelve; after that night, she never drove for her again. At least not to the Warbonnet. And their little brother never had to drive for their mother once.

And Arlen was the proudest son on the court at Senior Night.

STEW

ACT I

She made the best stew on the entire Rez.

Granted, it was a small Rez – a thousand people. Still, that's a lot of stew and amongst those thousand people, she was the very, very best. She took all of the parts of the fish that nobody else wanted – the cheeks, the heads, the eyeballs. Especially the eyeballs – that was her favorite part. That's what she made her stew out of. The so-called "leftovers." She called the special stew that she made "Fishhead Stew." Fishhead stew brought her back to the time before commodities. It brought her back to before white men regulated what Indians ate. Fishhead stew took her back to before people threw away the best parts of the fish. What a wasteful people we've become. We used to eat everything. The Creator gave us the whole fish – why wouldn't we eat the whole fish?

She came from an era when the "taste" sense was not necessarily connected to "sight" or even what was considered clean. Things were a little less hygienic back then in the kitchen, and the superficial sense of cleanliness that exists today wasn't so prevalent. Food didn't have all the hormones, mercury and other junk that now pollutes the insides of animals, but the exteriors tended to be slightly dirtier. Indeed, the "dirty" parts of the animals were usually the tastiest parts. For example, headcheese, kidneys, liver and sweetbreads – now considered "poor people's food" and/or leftovers – were some of the most treasured parts of the animals. Also, tripe was a treat during those hard times; any type of meat was really. That was back when food wasn't a thing of convenience and the waistlines showed it – people were much skinnier, and happier, on those rare occasions that they got meat. Even tripe.

She had fond memories of tripe – she remembered her family looked forward to those times when they had family tripe-cleaning sessions. The anticipation! She remembered that she and all of her little cousins would be so excited about these times – they'd eat it like candy, like when it was blackberry season! And the tripe wasn't meant to be too clean – she could clearly remember her grandpa yelling at her as she cleaned the tripe along the beach, "Don't get them guts too clean!! Don't get them guts too clean!!" The imperfections had flavor in them.

Just like the eyeballs.

She came from an era before Andrew Zimmern called this type of food "Bizarre Foods." No, eyeball stew and tripe weren't "bizarre" – they were just "food."

Fishhead stew brought her right back to when she was a little girl, some eighty years ago. Before this housing development of brightly colored HUD houses went up and before this tribe even had a tribal center.

Things were a lot different now than when she was a little girl. The young folks didn't eat tripe anymore. They didn't eat sweetbreads, livers or kidneys either. There was a pizza joint down by the water so they didn't have to. They sold tacos at the gas station. There was a casino now that had lots of food options. The young folks barely ate clams here anymore. They barely ate salmon, crab or oysters. They definitely never ate cockles or mussels.

But despite the changes that she's seen in the community, the changes to the landscape, environment and taste buds, one thing has remained largely the same on this small reservation. Everybody ate her fishhead stew. Even the young people.

The young people within the community wouldn't have eaten this fishhead soup from anybody else. Heck, they didn't even want to eat it from her, but they couldn't help it – it was like emo/self-indulgent rap music. They certainly didn't want to like it – it was slimy, nasty, a guilty pleasure. Fishhead stew was like a 40-year-old man liking a Miley Cyrus song; he hated to admit it, but when he was in the privacy of his car or in the airplane on his Bose headphones he loved it. Similarly, these young Native folks would never admit this love of fishhead soup to their non-Native friends; they barely admitted it to their Native friends.

But they loved this soup. Their white friends just wouldn't understand it – their parents didn't make them eat it when they were kids (the white kids' parents didn't make them eat anything – it seemed like those kids could always tell their parents what they were going to eat). The Native kids now were more like the white kids than ever before – they didn't really eat that much Indian food. But the fishhead stew was different; the eyeballs and the fishhead stew tapped into a special part of these kids' genetic memory that they didn't even recognize. It must have been a recessive gene, like the Native kid who shows up with blond hair and green eyes – but it was there.

Under normal circumstances, these modern Indian teenagers, with their skinny jeans and overly gelled-up hair, never wanted to touch anything even slightly slimy (except their goopy hair gel). They hated getting their hands dirty – that's a generational thing.

These kids were the first generation of Indian kids on the Rez that grew up not fishing off the dock and not collecting frogs and not finding baby crabs on the beach. Instead, this generation grew up with Guitar Hero and Nintendo DS. Sure, they paddled in the canoes a couple of times during the summer, but it was a thing of convenience. Every time after they paddled in the canoe they showered, anxious to get the salt and sweat off of their bodies and not at all interested in letting the salt permeate their beings like it did with their ancestors. For their ancestors, the salt was a part of their DNA, it ran deeply in their veins. Not these kids – they hated getting their hands and their bodies dirty. They always brushed their hands off on their skinny jeans when their hands got even slightly dirty.

Yet, they loved her fishhead soup. And they didn't even know why.

She sold her fishhead soup at the Farmers Market. She prepared bowls of the special soup and sold them for three dollars a bowl. She had a hand-drawn sign that said "Tina's Fishheads" – the sign showed evidence of her unsteady hand shaking as she wrote the letters. Still, despite her sometimes-unsteady hand, she was a nimble old lady – she rolled her dolly with a large pot of soup up there by herself. She set up her table – put the bowls, paper towels and spoons side by side – all by herself. Every Wednesday, those overly hygienic little

Indian kids would all run up the hill from the bus stop to the Farmer's Market to try her fishhead soup. They gladly gave of their scarce resources to get some of this very slimy, yet very tasty, treat.

The police station sat right across the street from the Farmer's Market. They always watched, with suspicion, anytime a large group of kids excitedly ran anyplace. Still, they knew not to mess with Ol' Tina – not because they never suspected her of anything. No, the Rez's finest checked her fishhead stew on many occasions to make sure that she wasn't packing any contraband in her recipe. They always had to specifically train the new officers not to go inspect her goods.

One of the young officers looked with particular suspicion at the gathering kids. The burly Sergeant directed his young officer, "Don't do it, Matthews. She's clean. I know it looks like there's something in there, but we've tested it over and over again."

The younger officer with "Matthews" on his name badge replied, "But Sarge, look at the way they're running up there. That's some 'Walking Dead'/'Breaking Bad' stuff. I'm telling you. Maybe it's not meth. But there's something.... Teenagers?? Running to get fishheads?? No, Sarge – I don't believe it."

Sarge took a sterner tone. "Don't even think about it, Matthews. Don't even try it. That's an order. You know how embarrassing it's been every single time an officer took samples of her stew? Then we have to deal with the anger...."

Matthews interrupted him, "But she's an old lady. How angry is she really going to get??"

Sarge smirked at him, "It's not her anger I'm worried about. Those kids will tear you apart for taking some of their precious stew. Don't do it."

Matthews begrudgingly listened. That old lady is up to something. He looked up the hill suspiciously, brow furrowed and eyes narrowed. She's definitely up to something.

ACT II

Matthews had been helping Tina bring her gear up to the top of the hill for about three months now. She never asked, but he made it a point to tell her that he was a "southern gentleman" – he figured that would be explanation enough for him wanting to help her. "We never even let a woman open a door for herself. Call me old-fashioned." He smiled at her charmingly. She smiled back at him and told him that his accent sounded like he was from Wisconsin. He couldn't lie to her. "I am actually from Wisconsin, ma'am. But I'm from southern Wisconsin."

She told him, "Sure. Thank you. I've been bringing my own stove and pots up here for the past twelve years. But I'll take some help."

Every Wednesday, Matthews kept looking for clues of some sort of narcotics going in the fishhead stew. Fortunately, the Rez was pretty low crime – he could afford to spend a little time staking out the Farmer's Market. Matthews watched her as she prepared the stew when they got to the Farmers Market. He put together the big picnic-style table for her and she laid out her ingredients. Potatoes, onions, coho salmon (the whole thing – even though it was called "fishhead stew," the whole fish actually went into it. Everything – fins, bones, etc), pepper, milk, fish stock, carrots and salt. There was also a small, silver, metal canister that had athletic tape wrapped around it and handwritten in red letters on the side, "Special."

Hmmmmmmm, Matthews thought, special what? Maybe THAT was the answer to this mystery. I need to figure out what's in that canister.

Miss Tina let the ingredients blend together for hours. Matthews wasn't a seafood eater, but he grew to love the smell of the stew. She stirred regularly, for about forty-five minutes, and then it was done. It would just simmer for the rest of afternoon, until the kids got out of school. Flavors blending together. Magic, alchemy. Matthews noted that she always put a big bowl on the table and would just let it sit there – she said that it was for her "grandfather." Matthews thought that must be a pet name for some old geezer that she liked to flirt with, and he just never came to get his food.

Matthews knew that this was entirely too early in his and Tina's relationship to ask her what was in the container. Even if it was, improbably, some innocent concoction, obviously no good, self-respecting chef is going to want to give away their special ingredients so easily. He knew that it wasn't that innocent – it wasn't simply a blend of twelve herbs and spices – but even if it were, he wasn't going to get it that easily.

After a few more months of helping Tina, she began to feel more comfortable making small talk with him. He'd ask her, "Miss Tina, why do you think those kids love your fishhead soup like they do?"

She smiled at him and replied, "Matthew, did I ever tell you that I have a great-nephew named Matthew? He isn't white though. And he's much better looking than you. And he works out more than you. But you remind me a lot of him."

The comment made Matthews slightly self-conscious; he'd been doing cross-fit for about six months and was feeling pretty good about his physique lately. He even started wearing a snug-fitting police uniform to show off his glutes and pecs a little more. Maybe he needed to get into the gym even more. Still, he knew that he couldn't let Tina know that his feelings were hurt. "Thank you, Miss Tina. I'm sure he's a handsome devil. Why do I remind you of him?"

Tina stood, stirring her stew. "You just do. You know, Matthew couldn't wait to get to my house to eat my fishhead stew when he was a kid. He always wanted to know what was in it. He told me, 'Auntie, you need to open your own restaurant – people will come from far and wide to eat your stew.' Matthew is a smooth talker. Like you, you southern Wisconsin gentleman. You are very sweet for a tribal police officer – most of the time you guys don't try to understand us."

She couldn't see Matthews at that moment – she was too busy stirring her stew. But she could feel the heat from his face as he blushed. Matthews knew that telling her a lie was pretty silly. Still, he had to figure out some excuse so that he could go investigate this stew. "Why was Matthew so sure that people would come from far and wide to eat your stew?"

Without missing a beat, she replied, "Because of the special ingredient. It's what everybody needs. Everybody needs their fix, whether they know it or not. I give them that. These kids today need it more than ever. They'll need it even more tomorrow. That's why they'll keep coming and even more will come tomorrow."

Is she about to tell me what she's putting in there? Finally. Sarge is going to be amazed at my police work when he realizes that I got her to confess without even interrogating her. I'm going to be employee of the month and probably get an end-of-the-year award named after me. The "Matthew Matthews Brilliant Investigation Award." Matthews' face lit up and the thought of his award motivated him to keep talking, asking even more questions. "So you think that they actually need it, Miss Tina?"

Tina laughed. "Of course they do!" she said with a big, beautiful smile on her weathered, brown skin. "Everybody needs it. That's why I keep that big, ol' dispenser right there – so I can pour large amounts in the stew and give everybody what they need. It's powerful – and the thing is, Matthew, that I have pretty much an endless supply. I can even put it in there and not charge anything if I really wanted to, but y'know, I like to have some extra spending money, too."

The Farmers Market came and went; another week, another sold-out pot of fishhead stew. The kids came up to the stand like fiends, got their fix, and then went off smiling in total bliss. Freakin' disgusting.

On the bright side, Matthews was pretty sure that he was making an airtight case. It's almost as if she wants to confess to me. I heard that criminals want people to know and find out, like Ray Liotta said in Goodfellas, "Only people that want to get caught go to jail." This is her cry for help. She's tired of polluting the community, the Rez, with this evil narcotic. He thought, next week is the week I bust her. I go catch her in the middle of preparing her container of secret drugs before the Farmers Market and bust her before she gets to mess these kids up any more.

ACT III

Today was the big day. Wednesday. Farmers Market day. Bust-The-Old-Lady-Day, Matthews thought. He knew what his game plan was – he was going to keep it hush-hush with Sarge. He didn't want Sarge busting his chops. He talked to Tina the week before and asked her if it was ok if he picked her up if it was windy outside. It was windy outside. Now, he had the perfect reason; he looked like a concerned community policeman, going over to Tina's house under the auspices of it being a little bit windy out. If the Sarge found out he was going over there, Matthews would just tell him that he didn't want any of her supplies blowing around. Matthews knew that once he was over at her house that she'd ask him in; he'd politely accept. Of course he'd accept – on the Rez, nobody refused offers from old ladies to go into their house.

Once there, he'd take a quick sniff around to see if the narcotic was foreign or domestic. Then he'd look around for possible hiding places and when she was grabbing the last of her supplies, he'd make his move. She couldn't possibly hide it all that well – she did say that she had pretty much a limitless supply! He was going to look in the most obvious places first – under the sink, in the refrigerator, garbage can, etc.

He got to her house and went up the walk to the door. He took a deep breath. This is going to be my first big bust – be cool. Be cool. Breathing, slow down. He took another deep breath. Cool. He knocked on the door. Not too loud – he didn't want to knock like he was there to bust her. This wasn't that sort of action – bad PR. Gotta be respectful of the old folks here on the Rez. Even if it's being respectful when I bust them! He grinned at the thought. He knocked again.

Nobody answered.

He knocked again. Nothing. She knew that I was coming over. I wonder what's going on? He hollered through the door, "Miss Tina?" He waited a few moments, "MISS TEEN-UH???" He got progressively louder.

That's weird. Maybe even suspicious. He knew that he didn't have probable cause to enter her house, but he really did believe that criminals wanted to get caught. Maybe she set this up and allowed herself to be in a position where he could catch her? He let his TJ Hooker instinct take over; this was his chance. He jiggled the door handle. It was unlocked – she wants to get caught, he kept on thinking.

He crept through the door, looking around. Like many HUD houses, the living room and then kitchen were the first rooms that a person saw when they walked in, straight ahead. You got to the bedroom by taking a left right before you got to the kitchen. There was nothing in the kitchen or the living room. He knew that if she were getting her food ready, she would be in the kitchen getting her spices together. Instead, she was someplace else, probably getting her real goodies together.

He heard something. A whisper. It sounded like a cry. It came from the left, toward where the bedrooms were. Now he was getting a bit more suspicious – he put his hand on his gun just in case. I heard these old Indian ladies are pretty tough. He crept quietly – almost noiselessly – down the hallway ready to spring into action just in case he saw her with her stash. He developed his story while he stalked down the hallway; he knew that there would be questions about whether or not he had probable cause. He planned to counteract that by saying that he was concerned for the old lady's safety when she didn't respond. "I thought it was one of those "I've fallen and I can't get up" situations. When I got to the end of the hallway, I see this old lady in a stash of meth." Meth was heavy on his mind because he'd been watching the Breaking Bad marathon; he knew she probably wasn't putting meth in her stew, but he just thought it made his bust sound a little bit more badass.

He got to the end of the wall and saw her leaning over a table, with her "special" container in front of her. This is it! He had her. He knew he had her. He was trying to listen a bit closer so that he could hear what was going on. He could barely see the container – caught her in the freakin' act!!

It was perfectly quiet in the house other than Miss Tina. He could hear her crying. He could hear the tears dripping loudly:

"Grandfather, please help these poor kids remember who they are and where they come from. I humbly ask you to help this fishhead stew trigger the ancestors within them. We need it to make them want to learn more about our ways of life – our people lived by these ways of life and died for this way of life. It's beautiful. Grandfather, it is so important for those precious kids to remember who they are – they are Indian kids, not just any kids. They come from poor yet strong people, people who lived through the worst of times and still always smiled. Grandfather, our people could smile in bad times because of family and love and...food. We are powerful people, they are powerful kids. They are not meant to be like every other kid – I hear these young folks talk about "we're still here" and "represent," Grandfather...they don't need to represent or remind anybody that they are still here. They need to stop worrying about how they look to everyone else – that's why they're more worried about their hair and shoes and clothes than they are about speaking their language or going to ceremonies. We were not vain people – we didn't care about representing and showing people we were still here. Other people knew we were because of the way we took care of our own community, not because of the t-shirts we wore or earrings we wore. We were one people. We took care of each other. We fed each other, somehow. Grandfather, you gave us food and we made stew. Please help my cooking help these kids remember how important stew is to our people. You gave us stew to show that our people could make beauty and perfection and something very desirable out of what other people call the "scraps." We've always done that. Please continue to bring these poor, lost kids to the meaning of the stew and understand that our way of life is all about making beauty of nothingness. We make do with nothing and make it taste perfect, make it taste like love. I love those kids so much and want them to understand how beautiful our ways of life are.

Aho. You know I love these kids."

Matthews watched Miss Tina bottle up the tears in her "special" container. He started crying, too. He wasn't crying because he suspected the old lady of being a drug dealer – that made sense. What she gave out was addictive. But he was crying because he only had a job because Miss Tina was right – the community does not take care of each other anymore. If it did, he becomes irrelevant and doesn't need to be around.

Matthews continued to help her with her Wednesday Farmers Market fishhead stew cooking. He wasn't sure that it was going to help the kids find that piece of "Indianness" that was needed for the community members to start taking care of each other again, to start acting like a "tribe again" – he didn't know. Still, it was a start. Plus, he loved the contented look the kids got when they ate Miss Tina's fishhead stew. It looked like they tasted a bit of the past, a bit of history, and it made so much sense to them.

Matthews watched those kids communicate. It was always different during the time they ate their stew. For those five or ten minutes of eating that fishhead stew (and maybe five or ten minutes afterwards), those kids knew exactly who they were and ate with their ancestors.

(This story is for every single Native woman who makes a miracle happen and spices up their recipes with love, tears and prayer.)

CRADLEBOARD:
THE BALLAD OF DUSTIN AND ELAINE

Chapter I
MEETING DUSTIN

First time I saw **Dustin**
We were in class
Converse cleats
Hoodie and braces
He fell down next to my desk
First day of seventh grade
Tripped
Untied laces
Looked up
Face red
Smiled
Chunks and traces
Of the corndogs we had for lunch
In his teeth
It was disgusting

But **Dustin** *was so, so sweet.*

He said "Hi."

I smiled back at him.

Shook my head
Told him, "We learned to tie our shoes
In second grade.
I think you may have missed your chance."
He picked his books up
Flipped his braids
Back over his shoulder
With a swing of his neck
He was unafraid

Flashed the goofiest smile
Full of metal
That I ever saw before.

I spoke to him
Trying not to laugh
And blush at the same time.
*I said, "Hi. My name is **Elaine**."*

Chapter II
NOT WITHOUT MY FRIEND

*A girl from 8th grade Science class invited **Elaine** to a party*
Popular girl
Lived on a lake
*Told **Elaine** that she could stay the night*
If she happened to be over too late
The girl was a "cool" girl
A white girl
A rich girl
In a school where the cool, white and the rich
Usually cared not about Indians
They never came out to our rez
They never understood why the cute Indian girls only wore
A memorial basketball tourney hoodie
Red basketball gear galore
Basketball shoes and shorts everyday
Those white, popular kids just usually ignore.
They don't ask any questions
They don't really even want to know
*I don't have a clue what made the white girl talk to **Elaine** in Science class*
*I couldn't think of any reason why **Elaine** wouldn't want to go.*

*This was **Elaine's** chance to be noticed.*
To be someone more than Indian.
More than a girl with chipped nail polish
Whose mother never came

To the parent teacher conferences
Where she dropped her head in shame
Just another Indian girl who wished that one of the white ladies there
was her mom
All of us just wanted to be seen as the same
Wanted to be seen as more than the poor girl who tried hard
More than just the Indian girl with the weird last name.

But she wasn't.
Yet
This was her chance to be more.
Elaine *did the weirdest thing in the world right then.*
She pointed at me sitting alone in the back of the science class
And
*Told the popular girl, "I'll go only if my friend **Dustin** can come."*

Chapter III
DUSTIN'S JOURNAL ENTRY

We kept each other standing tall
Completely secure swaddled in each other's friendship
As we matured

Elaine *taught me about the girls who would one day want a good man*
But right now could not appreciate one properly
She told me to see past a sad story
Don't be the person making everything right
"You can't save anybody
They've got to want to save themselves."
She taught me to always take inventory
Of intention

She said,
*"**Dustin,** most of them don't deserve you."*

To which I replied,
"Then how come they don't want me?"

She told me,
"Because their tastes are not refined."
Then she'd stick out her tongue and say "ayyyyyyyzzzz"
We'd crack up laughing
Me cackling and her snorting combined.

Then we'd fall asleep sitting up
Her back pushed against mine keeping each other straight.
Only a sheet wrapped around us tightly
Human cradleboard
Comfort and
Good dreams innate.

Not even dreaming or thinking about what we couldn't afford or how
we didn't know what we were gonna do with the rest of our lives.

Chapter IV
ELAINE'S JOURNAL ENTRIES

After a year of staying home and just existing
No jobs to be had
We decided that we would go to Haskell together
Dustin *played ball and I got into theater*
Got into my culture
I never wanted to be white again
Never worried about my mom not showing up
Learned from the other Skins
Learned about other Nations
Which tribes have the finest men
Also
The dances
The songs
The way that other Natives carry on
Every single step of the way
Dustin *came along*
My brown knight in starchy wranglers
Rescuing me from awkward pauses with creepy guys at parties

Keeping me strong
When I wanted to leave
Homesick
Grieving
Grandpa dying that week
I had no money to go back home
Dustin *told me to keep on believing*
This was what grandpa wanted
"Honor him with your grades."
I cut my hair the day he passed
When I saw ***Dustin*** *an hour later*
He had cut off his braids.

I was shocked
Angry at first
Asked him, "What did you do??"

He told me with tears in his eyes:
"If I cannot mourn with you, ***Elaine***
Who can I mourn with?"

God sent me the best friend in the world.

Poetic.
Soon after ***Dustin*** *cut his hair*
Girls began to notice his chiseled face
I told him it was just a matter of time
Next thing he tells me that this really cool girl is coming to his place
To pick him up to go to the movies
Dollar movies
Cheap date
Dustin *says,*
*"Her name is "****Grace****.""*

He told me that ***Grace*** *is special*
She doesn't drink
She doesn't smoke or get
Jealous when other girls
Ask him for help with calculus

She knows he's smart
And doesn't throw a fit.
She's a homebody
Watches Grease
Working on her English Lit

I told him that she sounds awesome,
Dustin
"She looks kinda chubby
Why is her stomach so big?"

I was the first to tell him "congratulations."
Even bought him a blue cigar.
I was slightly jealous
Still I meant it
I know that he's going to be the best dad in the world
And
I'm going to be right there to babysit
And
*Lighten his and **Grace's** load.*

Although
There's a part of me that feels like
That load should be mine.

Chapter V
OBLIVIOUS

__Elaine__ was such a natural actress
Each facial expression held a thousand pictures
A million words
She was always on the brink
The next big thing
Dreams deferred
Shakespeare Festivals every summer
Spam and Top Ramen at night
But she was living her dream.
We were ten years out of college

She was a welcome visitor to our living room
Suddenly
Tears began to stream

Like any man when he sees a woman crying
I don't know what it means
All I knew was I wanted to calm her down
Fix the situation by any means
I told her "I only saw happy pictures of you in San Francisco!"

Elaine *told me, "Things aren't always what they seem."*

Chapter VI
THE TRUTH

We all sat on couches catching up and drinking coffee
Elaine, Dustin *and I*
Dustin *and I were startled when* ***Elaine*** *began to cry*
But this was ***Dustin's*** *friend*
His sister
So I grabbed some Kleenex to dry her eyes
She was grateful
Gracious
Smiled at me
And touched my cheek
Took a deep breath
Closed her eyes
Before she began to speak
Told us that we may want to sit down
She's got something to get off her chest:

So we sat down.

And ***Elaine*** *said:*
"Here I am an educated Native woman
Age 33
Overqualified for most Native guys
From what me and my friends see

My Daddy showed me that most Indian men lie
When he left mom and I
So why would I trust someone who looks like me?
Still
I want little spiky haired tykes
With funny names just like
You two have,

Dustin *and* **Grace.**

Yet
The truth is that the
Only Indian man that I ever gave the same chance
That I gave to every other race of men
Romantically
Never even made an advance

He is the exception
To my scrutiny of sliding scale expectations
That is raised several degrees
Whenever Native men are the topic
Barely gave any a meaningful chance

Therefore
I have no basis to keep saying it
Still
I just cannot seem to stop saying it
I gave so many other men much more of a chance
But
I convinced myself and just cannot stop saying it
Even though I know it's not true

"There are no good Indian men."
"There are no good Indian men."
"There are no good Indian men."

The only exception
Is you
Dustin.*"*

"Please pardon my honesty
Grace
Since he met you
There's never been a doubt in my mind
That he's yours
And not mine
I have no delusions of grandeur
I'm glad you two are happily together
Both of you made quite a find
But since I judge everyone by my dad
I found that I'm quite a few years behind
Now I'm in a bind and desperate
My finances are fine
My professional qualifications are strong
My resume is divine
But I'm cynical and suspicious
Too smart to get knocked up
The irony is rich and unkind
Still
I'm too close to barren lands
Please bear that in mind
With no real prospects on the horizon
I cannot be prideful or silent or let questions go unasked
No matter how stupid it might sound
So I'll just ask

Grace
Can I borrow my best friend's seed?
I understand if you want to smack me
Or if you want me to leave
But I had to ask
Can I borrow my best friend's seed?"

Chapter VII
CONTENT

"I'm so proud of you
Grown woman

You are a sight to behold
True Indigenous
No wrinkles
No crow's feet, fine lines or folds
Nature's pearl cream
You are a pedophile's dream
Except I know you'd beat that ass.

Truth be told
Elaine
Other than the grey hair and the glasses
You look exactly like
You did when we were 20 years old

Except now
Your handsome teenage son gives away your age.

I remember how you carried him in his cradleboard:
Single mother graceful
With elegance
Maternal spirit
Intelligence
That allows you to raise your teenage son alone
He's grown up calling me "uncle."
Still
You made sure he's always understood how you and I
Worked together to help create
A miracle made in a lifetime of love
He knows that he was fate
A perfect, almond-eyed, spiky-haired miracle
Before it was too late
You told him

"Although he cannot see you every day
He will help keep your back straight
Security wrapped around you tightly
Human cradleboard
Love innate."
He's your cradleboard.

SUTRO

INTRO/FIERCE

"There is a need to approach Western people as a contaminated people, regardless of color or heritage – Indians are not exempt from that disease...these people are ill, but only they can help themselves...they must want treatment and be willing to give up some of the pleasures gained from their disease."

John Mohawk, Western Peoples, Natural Peoples, Thinking in Indian

"In the old times...people were pretty strict. Today, you young people think that because no one guides you in making decisions, that this is better because you think you are free to make decisions for yourself. But you are not free – rather, you are lost."

John Mohawk, We Are by Nature Social Animals, Thinking in Indian

"To return to love, to get the love we always wanted but never had, to have the love we want but are not prepared to give, we seek romantic relationships. We believe these relationships, more than any other, will rescue and redeem us. True love does have the power to redeem but only if we are ready for redemption. Love saves us only if we want to be saved."

"Contrary to what we may have been taught to think, unnecessary and unchosen suffering wounds us but need not scar us for life. It does mark us. What we allow the mark of our suffering to become is in our own hands."

bell hooks, All About Love: New Visions

She was Indian, right? So this was like a new tradition. All Indians had traditions. Right? This was what they call "walking in two worlds." She heard about Indians walking in two worlds. This was like a modern greeting-the-morning-sun ceremony. She envisioned generations and generations of Native ancestors, if they had the capability to do so, doing this.

She had to be at work by eight. Work was thirteen minutes away. Traffic in Nashville was pretty bad this time of the morning. Still, it was 7:25 now. Plenty of time.

She looked at her cracked phone screen for a good thirty seconds. Different angles, making different faces. She sucked in her cheeks, narrowed her eyes, arched her eyebrows. She made herself look as cherub-like as she could. Pretty soon that initial thirty seconds turned into minutes; she had her commute down to a science, "I can leave in ten minutes and still make it on time." Then "I can leave in five minutes and still make it on time if traffic is good." She knew that traffic would be good – she wouldn't be late. She was only a few seconds away from the perfect shot.

Ten minutes went by, then twenty – all spent on making different sorts of expressions and looking into the phone screen.

Her features were flawless. To say her skin was brown would be an understatement. She had almond brown skin with that the reddish tint of copper; no matter what anybody thought about the term or the sports team, she made the term "redskin" make perfect sense. She was a redskin in the very best possible way – she had the reddest of brown skins that hearkened back to a day before so-called discovery, when all Natives had beautiful, reddish-brown skin. Her skin looked lush – almost liquid – it was so even and perfect. Her skin looked like it could be a yummy fruit smoothie that you could drink. Her eyes were dark brown and almond shaped...but very skinny almonds. She talked with a squint, a glint to her eyes that happened naturally. She didn't have to stage it. She was about 5'8", but because of her penchant for heels (open-toed, that always showed her perfectly French-manicured toes), she looked closer to 5'10" or 5'11".

She had strong, black hair that looked like it belonged on Filipina women deep in the bush of the Philippines; it was medusa-like and seemed to have a life of its own. It went down to the small of her back. Perfectly manicured real fingernails, a cream silk blouse, an orange pencil skirt. She was the prototypical slick, "woman of the new millennium"-type Native woman remixed with the romanticized version of a "Pocahontas"-type Indigenous "princess" that many Native women looked like before skin and hair and features were Europeanized by intermarriage, before Native people changed to the high-starch diet forced upon them by Europeans, and before Natives moved from a hunter/gatherer diet and food became a thing of convenience. She had the type of body that nature required Native women to have in order to survive well before "commod bods" became the norm. Taut, lean and muscular – survival wouldn't allow soft, doughy or obese bodies during hunter/gatherer times.

She was a cosmopolitan-ass, hunter/gatherer, Indigenous bush woman of the new millennium. She was stunning.

Still, for some reason she was gun-shy about taking this particular picture. It seemed like it pained her to pull the trigger on the camera. It must have been an evolutionary response, a behavior learned over generations and generations of taking pictures with actual film cameras. "That shit costs money." She was only 22; certainly she never used a film camera and didn't know how much it cost to develop. Yet, she was cautious to actually take the picture. So instead of taking pictures, she just made faces at the screen, waiting for the perfect shot.

Got it. 7:55.

"Damn, I'm gonna be late again." she said to herself as she got into her car. "I hope I don't get fired." *The picture was worth it though*, she thought.

It was a pretty sweet picture. Perfect, in fact. Stoic. She never smiled in pictures because not smiling was much sexier. Mouth slightly agape. No hard creases, her eyes were squinting just a little bit (this was a bedroom-eyes trick she learned from watching Food

Network at her grandma's house – Giada De Laurentiis always had great squinting eyes that looked sexy!! Granted, Giada has a huge freakin' head compared to her body and short, chubby red fingers that looked like sausages, but her eyes were amazing), perfectly symmetrical. Lips were glossy; her MAC foundation and Instagram filter took away any bit of excess shine. This picture was sexy, but it looked like it was "effortless sexy." She posted the picture to her Instagram, Facebook and Twitter with the captions #Fierce, #NoFilter, #NativePride, #SexiestNative, #Navajo, #Italian, #Culinary, #Beauty, #Modest, #GoodEats, #Nashville, #Instagood and #Vegan. The truth was that she wasn't Navajo, Italian or vegan, but she knew that these hashtags would get her a few extra views from people who were either Navajo or vegan or followed those hashtags. Plus, she liked Giada a lot, and Giada was Italian and could cook her big head off. However, her "Native" hashtag was accurate as she was indeed Native, but she didn't know from where. In fact, if she knew more about Navajos (or Natives in general), she would realize that the notion of being a vegan Navajo was damn near an oxymoron.

Her "Nashville" hashtag was also accurate – she lived in the home of Country Music! She hated country music. She hated cowboy boots and cowboy hats. Nashville literally only had a handful of Native people living there, and so people in the area always thought she was Mexican, which she also hated. *All the more reason to stay inside and away from these rednecks.* She couldn't wait to end her workday and retreat from Country Music-ville to her cyber-home at 5 o'clock.

Her Instagram name was "Lovely Native Giada." She had a tattoo across her left breast that she showed off quite often in her pictures; that tattoo let everyone know that her real name was "Delilah." She really was quite lovely – brown-skinned, and didn't actually need all of the filters and makeup that she employed. But she loved them. Plus, with five-thousand Twitter followers, a few thousand friends on Facebook and over thirty-thousand followers on Instagram, she was now officially an internet celebrity – one of the only Native internet celebrities – and so she knew that her adoring public demanded perfection. So she gave them perfection; her favorite filter was called "Sutro," because she thought that it made her look deep and introspective. She wasn't just another pretty face. That was important.

She was deep. All the dudes who commented on her Facebook posts told her so. She'd write, "I may not be a size two or a model but I know that I'm beautiful inside and out!" and one hundred and twenty guys would like it and about half of them would comment and tell her how she is so brave and smart for making that post.

Of course they never met her and the reason that they initially followed her was because she had a tendency to show a lot of cleavage. But they nonetheless knew that she was brave.

Of course she knew that she had a lot to offer. There was no question about that. After all, every single one of the memes that she reposted said so. Like the meme that said, "I'm not a one-in-a-million kind of girl, I'm a once-in-a-lifetime kind of woman." When that one first came across her iPhone screen, her eyes lit up. It was early in her workday in a new temping position and she was dedicated to letting her boss know that she was the right one for this job. While sitting at her desk, halfway sorting the morning mail and halfway checking her Tweets, she actually said it out loud, "Wow, that is so real! I know, right?! That's SO me. I am a once in a lifetime woman!" The temps in this particular office didn't get cubicles. The lack of privacy allowed Delilah's coworker sitting to her right, a non-smart phone user named "Betty," (Delilah once commented that Betty should get a backpack for her phone) to spy on her and take note of all the photo shoots and social networking that she did on company time.

Betty later covertly reported Delilah's extensive photo shooting and social media use to their supervisor – payback for the "backpack" comment. Betty wanted to tell Delilah off, but wasn't able to think of any really catty comebacks in the moment. The next day she thought, I should have told her, *"At least my phone doesn't have a yeast infection from taking coochie shots!"* Since Betty couldn't think of anything good to say, she decided the next best course of action was to get Delilah fired. Betty told the supervisor that she'd be damned if she's going to be doing all the morning mail sorting while someone right next to her is getting inspired. This job isn't about being inspired – it's about temping.

Sometimes once-in-a-lifetime women get backlash. Hating.

But Delilah continued to be inspired anyway. In fact, she was inspired right up until the moment that she was called into the supervisor's office. When she got the email to come to the supervisor's office, she was completely unaware of Betty's snitching. She didn't know what the meeting was about – she thought maybe she was getting a promotion. She took an Instagram photo of her sharp, businesswoman outfit and hashtagged it #DressedForSuccess, #Fierce, #NoFilter, #NativePride, #SexiestNative, #Navajo, #Italian, #Culinary, #Beauty, #Modest, #GoodEats, #Nashville, #Instagood and #Vegan.

The supervisor told her that she was a bit too inspired for this company and that she should turn in her key-swipe card immediately. She did. She was shocked that she was let go – *what the heck just happened??* Still, she was inspired. She wasn't going to allow a little thing like unemployment rain on

I AM NOT A ONE IN A MILLION KIND OF GIRL... I'M A ONCE IN A LIFETIME KIND OF WOMAN.

her beautiful day. "I'm a once in a lifetime woman" she would often say during her morning photo shoots. *All of my fans know that. That's why they follow me. They wouldn't follow me unless I knew the way.*

She didn't smile in pictures. *Fierce!! Gotta be fierce!!* It was almost as if she was mad at the camera, mad at her followers – she looked fierce. However, the thought of people following her made her smile. *They follow me. I've got to lead them someplace good.* That was a big responsibility.

There wasn't a lot of money in being an internet celebrity. In fact, it cost her a lot of money, if anything – she's been fired from three temp jobs for using too much company time taking pictures of herself. She wasn't overly concerned about the money – she could always go back to school. She seemed to be carefree; she was fortunate like that. Plus, she was pretty convinced that it was only a matter of time before her celebrity led to a modeling contract or a singing contract from one of her *a cappella* videos. But even if it didn't lead to any of those things, she had a duty to make herself available to her followers; she provided a service. They gained inspiration from her everyday life, and so she had to give that to them to keep them going and happy. She had a mission.

If a supervisor couldn't see that and accommodate it, well then he's simply not the right boss for a once in a lifetime woman like her.

MIRRORS

It was 9:39 a.m. Tuesday, she was pretty sure. She checked the calendar. *Yep, September 15th. Four weeks. Shit! Four weeks. I don't want to have to tell Mom and Dad, but I'm going to have to pretty soon, to even get some food. My phone's supposed to be shut off when?*

Delilah used her palms to wipe her eyes and moved her hands over cheeks until her fingers covered her nose and her palms covered her mouth. Hands firmly in her face. After her vision cleared, she looked at her palms and saw the mascara on them. "Yuck."

She said to no one in particular, "Dammit, I didn't mean to sleep this late." She'd been sleeping this late for the past three weeks, but she felt like she needed to get back on a schedule. Just in case. This was her fourth week of being jobless. This time. It was like a three-month cycle: 1) get a job, 2) get enamored with the job, 3) have a falling out with a coworker over Facebook or email, 4) get fired. This time was the worst though – she didn't save up much money before she got fired and things were getting pretty lean.

Delilah didn't want to, but she made herself keep her eyes open. Immediately upon sitting up, she grabbed her phone on the side of the bed. She put in her code, 4321, and checked her Instagram, Twitter and Facebook in that order. She got out of bed and lit up some sweetgrass and kinnickkinnick. Her morning ritual. She put the burning embers into a large abalone shell. *I love the way this stuff smells.* She carried the abalone shell with the burning incense as she went into the bathroom – it was still dark. She sat the shell on the bathroom counter and looked up at the mirror. She made it a point to look at the mirror in the dark before turning the bathroom light on – nothing.

This time she left the light off.

These jobless, hungry times always made her more introspective and post more mirror shots instead of simply pointing the camera toward herself. "Selfies." She thought that the mirrors added a spiritual element to her photos. Granted, she still liked to take the selfies, but when she was jobless she also took these mirror shots. She read that Indians once thought that mirrors had spiritual importance, like portals. Her friend Lisa confirmed that they were portals – plus, Lisa told her about the medicinal power they had. Delilah wondered if she really believed that, or if she just wanted to say that she believed that to feel "more Indian?" In either event, during these times of unemployment, her first photoshoot in the morning was not the same as the show she gave when she was employed. No, during this time, she wanted to show her deeper, more spiritual side – she prayed a lot. She wanted to show it. She took pictures of the bathroom mirror in the dark. She was earnest. She thought that the spirit in the mirror – if there was one – might have some answers for her.

>click<

Nothing. Well, not quite "nothing," but pretty darn close. The picture was black. You could barely see faint traces of the light illuminating from her bedroom lamp in the background. Still, it was pretty much black. It looked just like a picture of a dark room with no flash in the mirror. She posted it on Facebook, Twitter and Instagram.

People never really commented on these photos. Not even Lisa. As a matter of fact, she never got one single comment on them. Why would anybody? Delilah showed no cleavage in these shots, none of her tattoos or her lips or any part of her face. These pictures were just dark. She posted them and hashtagged them with different hashtags than her other photos, too, #JobHunting, #Spirits, #Mirrors, #SpiritualSelfie, #GhostDancing, #Native, #Navajo and #Guidance. Kind of weird. Still, she was used to getting massive amounts of likes and comments for every single photo – she even got a lot when she didn't put herself into the pictures, simply because some of the commenters wanted to show that they weren't just after her body and looks. For example, when she posted a picture of a puppy or a kid, men would comment about how cute the puppy or kid was and how they were dog/kid lovers just in case that puppy/kid was something that meant a lot to her. Commenting on the cute puppies/kids was some sneaky, G-14 classified form of flirting with hopes that she would consider them as a good candidate for fatherhood (or joint custody of a hound).

But nobody ever commented on her bathroom photos.

She rolled her eyes. She said one of her mantras out loud – something as important to her as the words of Sitting Bull or Chief Sealth, "I am a once in a lifetime woman." If they couldn't appreciate her once in a lifetime-ness, as expressed through pictures of a dark room, then they simply would not be the "one." Perhaps that's the guidance that she was getting from these dark photos – exactly who was not really in her corner?

Their loss. She put away her camera and got dressed for the day. She had to go spend some time meeting with some people at the unemployment office at eleven o'clock. *Time to get some money. Being broke sucks.*

TOILET PAPER

"Delilah Abernathy?" A very droll, unenthused female voice called out. About 15 seconds passed.

"Delilah Abernathy?" The bored voice called out again.

Delilah had been sitting on a hard, old and torn vinyl chair in a storefront room. The rows of chairs were chained together as if someone might steal them. She was looking at her phone's screen, checking her various social media networks. She didn't hear the voice the first time the lady called. The second time, she put down her phone as if she was in trouble and glided up to the source of the voice at the counter.

She tried to drum up enthusiasm. "G'morning!" She forced a fake smile at the unimpressed Unemployment Insurance receptionist. "My name is...oh yeah, you know my name. Well, I got this notice in the mail that I was 'posed to come in here and go through my interview for unemployment."

The expressionless secretary stared at Delilah. She wasn't wearing glasses, but if she were, she would have them down at the end of her nose, peering over the top of them at Delilah. "Yes, I know. I sent the letter. Do you have the items that I told you to bring in?"

"I do. Yes. I have um, my social security number, the names, business mailing addresses and telephone numbers of all my employers, um... my pay stubs. What else? Oh yeah, I've been contacting places trying to get interviews." Delilah smiled up at the lady, appearing satisfied that she was prepared. "That's it, right?"

The lady looked unimpressed.

"We don't require that you contact anybody for an interview. Yet. You don't get brownie points." The receptionist furrowed her brow when she looked at the computer screen on her desk, presumably looking at Delilah's history. "Miss Abernathy, why do you lose so many jobs? You seem to have a pattern here. It's not an official policy, but in my experience – and keep in mind that I've been here over 12 years – every time you come in here again, it decreases the odds of you being awarded unemployment benefits."

Delilah looked concerned. The receptionist continued.

"It's like a man who always tells you that his girlfriend is crazy, Miss Abernathy, even though he's been with about six different girlfriends. After some period of time you begin to see what the common denominator is – him. Generally, if everyone thinks this guy is a scumbag, every single one of them can't be wrong. It's probably him."

Delilah moved her head back in disbelief and her voice got quiet and high-pitched. "Are you calling me crazy?"

The receptionist continued calmly. "Not at all, Miss Abernathy. That was simply an analogy. I'm merely pointing out the limitations of our officers reviewing the claims. Right, wrong or indifferent – they usually think that where there's smoke, there's fire."

Delilah could not help but feel offended. Still, she understood, begrudgingly, what the lady was saying. Her mouth was open, wanting to have a snappy retort, but none came out. Instead, she tilted her head to the side as the receptionist handed her a number. 76. "The board will show you when your number comes up. There is coffee in the back of the room. Thank you, Miss Abernathy."

Delilah went to the back of the room. She knew that she got told off, but in an incredibly polite and, frankly, correct way. She was seething as she stirred powdered cream into her coffee. *I hope this fills me up for a little while.* She pulled out her phone and opened up her Instagram account. *Still no comments on that picture. Nobody liked it. Shallow people.* She looked at the picture again. There must have been something going on with the fluorescent lighting in this office – there was a burst of light cutting across the screen. She adjusted the phone from side to side to try to get rid of it. *I hate fluorescent lights. No wonder this shit drives dogs epileptic. They probably get frustrated looking at their phones with this stuff on.*

Epileptic dogs. Her mind continued to wander. *Who the hell cares if a dog is epileptic? I've seen Indians post on Facebook about "rez dogs" – that they're wild and beautiful because of their desperation. I bet there are no epileptic rez dogs..*

She smiled at that thought.

She looked up at the number board, illuminated with red numbers. *Damn, they're only on 52. Maybe I'll catch a quick nap.* She sat and observed for awhile – maybe three minutes. The board remained on 52. She took inventory of how long it took for the numbers to come up – finally, about another three minutes later, the numbers changed, "Now calling number 53." She did some quick math in her head. *At this pace, it'll take about a good hour. 15-minute nap.* She set her alarm. It was 11:23 now – *I'll set the alarm for 11:45.*

She got up to go the bathroom really quick. The coffee was moving through her at a pretty good rate – don't need any accidents at the unemployment line! She smiled broadly at the thought.

Delilah put down a few layers of toilet seat protectors. She put toilet paper in the bowl of the toilet so it didn't splash up at her. She got comfortable and began to enjoy evacuating her system.

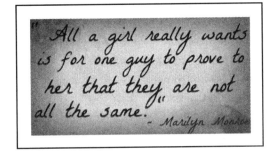

As she sighed with relief, she started the process of updating her Facebook while seated on the toilet (it was a process because the internet seemed to take forever in this cursed building). Her update read: All a girl really wants is for one guy to prove to her that they are not all the same. She always liked that meme. She posted an older picture of her self – one that she was saving for a rainy day – along with the quote and waited for the responses to come in. The picture had absolutely nothing to do with the meme; the picture was of her in a mini-skirt that she tried on at Macy's. She couldn't afford to buy it, so she tried it on and went upstairs to the bed section with it on. She posed provocatively on the bed – neither the skirt nor the bed being hers – by laying back and crossing her legs, and the skirt hiked up a bit. Her glistening brown legs (she knew that she was going to have this photo shoot, so she oiled her legs up before going there), combined with the "come and get it" expression on her face definitely was intended to appeal to the prurient nature in men. Sexy.

With the meme, apparently she wanted a guy to prove that they're not all the same by not being interested in this photo. She didn't understand that disinterest is the hardest thing to show on social networking – the whole structure is intended to only show when one is interested.

In either event, the "likes" and comments began flowing immediately. Within three minutes – while she was still sitting on the toilet, not getting splashed – she refreshed three times and on the third "refresh" the tally was up to seventy-two likes.

As usual, some of her better social media friends quickly responded to the picture by making statements about how they were proud to be her friend. There was one girl who responded to the picture with "LOL." Snarky. She was immediately blasted by Delilah's adoring/lustful legions of men who all chimed in in agreement to the meme. She seemed to always create consensus among men – not an easy feat (her best social media friend, and honestly her best friend, period, Lisa, liked to joke that she could have taken Delilah to Lisa's tribe's all-male tribal council and instantly solved about half the tribal council disputes). Delilah smiled at the thought of Lisa's homespun/Native wisdom – but the smile only lasted a brief moment. She took about 45 squares of the translucent, cheap, prosciutto-like, commercial-grade toilet paper *(why don't they just get some Charmin?)* to wipe her butt. She stood up and made sure that none of the toilet seat protectors stuck to her butt. *That'd be embarrassing.* She began to get a bit upset. Usually she would take this sort of response to a picture in stride – *they're my followers, they're supposed respond like this.* But in light of the complete lack of response to her earlier "spiritual" photo, this made her mad. *I'm a once in a lifetime kind of woman!! They only respond when I'm looking sexy? Fuck that.* She was going to try it again – see if there was a similar complete lack of response. She pulled her pants up and again refreshed to see how many likes and comments the picture had. One hundred and twenty-eight "likes," thirty-two comments. *Even if they don't really like those spiritual photos, they could at least comment or like them to thank me for consistently giving them content and pieces of my life!*

She was seething. She was planning on setting a trap of sorts for her supposed followers. She wanted to see how shallow or committed to her they really were. This relationship simply cannot be as simple as "I show some skin and you get your jollies but don't get to know the real me." That would be a serious shock to her system. She washed her hands and straightened herself up – she still had to look professional for her meeting. She was taking way too long in here, but was still in plenty of time for her number to be called. *It's only 11:40. I don't have time for a nap but I'm kinda all awake now. Damn perverts woke me up. I'm gonna set them up in a trap as soon as I get home.*

She walked hastily toward the door to get back for her meeting with the unemployment officer. But right before she got there, she noted the deadbolt lock on the bathroom door. She thought, *I'm not even going to wait until I get home. I have three minutes left. I'm gonna give him a show – he just doesn't know it.* She turned the lock on the deadbolt and turned off the lights. *This is a lot darker than it is at home.* She literally could not see her hand in front of her face. She knew that the flash was off – she always kept it off, didn't want her face to shine up. She turned the light on briefly just so that she would know where the mirror was – she wanted a square-on shot. She aligned her feet directly in front of the mirror.

She took off her shirt. She took off her bra. *He's gonna love this shot. Even if he doesn't know it.*

>click<

When she pressed the little circle on her phone to snap the picture, there was a bright flash. Or, at least, she thought she saw a bright flash. *That's impossible,* she thought. The lights were off and she didn't see anybody come inside the bathroom – she was standing only about three feet from the door, directly in front of the wall mirrors. The unemployment office was very, very "storefront" – the layout was just like every other piece of cheap commercial real estate in the country. Push open the door and the paper towels were directly to the right of you on the wall. The mirror was a bit further to the right, with two bland sinks and liquid hand soap dispensers built into the sinks. To the left of those sinks and mirrors are two bathroom stalls, with the handicapped access stall furthest to the left.

She knew nobody walked in because she was standing right beside the door. Besides, hadn't she engaged the deadbolt?

And she also knew that the flash couldn't have come from the phone/ camera. She never, ever used the flash on her trusty camera phone. She's adamant about that – she understands lighting probably better than most professional photographers from her daily photo shoots. She knows when and where she looks good, and which is her good side, etc. She likes those soft, environmentally friendly lights. They tended to take away the shine (and she just felt more relaxed there – she sweated less there). She hated fluorescent lights. She HATED, even more, too much sunlight – her skin got shiny and greasy-looking like Alicia Keys or Jermaine Jackson. And, even more than fluorescent lights or too much sunlight or camera-less cell phones, she hated camera flashes. Flashes seemed to find every single crevice, bump or line in her face. A camera flash on her face was like a black light on a cheap hotel bed – it exposes all the nasty little secrets and probably could tell some interesting stories. A camera flash on her face is like Sarah Jessica Parker without all the designer clothes – it exposes her as someone not nearly as hot as she likes to think she is.

It's safe to say that she didn't like camera flashes.

And that's precisely why she was positive that she didn't have the flash on when she took the picture just a few moments ago. *But then where in the hell did that light come from?* She looked around. It was still dark in there. *Maybe it was my eyes adjusting to the dark. Those blinky, star things that happen when you first open your eyes....* She figures that she must have just anticipated a flash, the same way that a person anticipates a kick when they shoot a gun. The sound of the camera click must have subconsciously made her think that there was a flash in this complete darkness. She anticipated it. She couldn't see, but her eyes were still somehow seeing shapes and colors from the imagined flash; she knew it was not real, but it was freaky nonetheless. She reached for the wall directly to her right, looking for the light switch. She fiddled around on the wall, bumped into the paper towel dispenser. She knew that the light switch was directly to the right of that, right by the door. She finally found the light switch and turned it on blindly. Her slowly eyes adjusted to the newly turned-on fluorescent light and she reached for the deadbolt. This time she really did see stars and so she grabbed blindly at the sink counter at her shirt and bra. *Gotta put my clothes back on. Walk out here with no damn shirt on and my boobs showing.* After a few grabs, she successfully retrieved it and put it on. She was pretty disheveled and so grasping the deadbolt was not nearly as easy as it should have been. The deadbolt was stuck. *Shit! How long have I been in here? They're probably on my number.* She jostled some more. She rolled her eyes at herself, completely unimpressed by her lack of forethought. *Yeah, this makes sense – how many people actually want to lock themselves in the unemployment office's bathroom? This isn't really the bathroom that you want to spend a lot of time in.* On the third attempt, she finally got the deadbolt to turn and she pushed the door firmly. It poofed open, as if it were excited to be unstuck. She exited hastily, but still mindful of her appearance – she didn't want to look like a crazy woman rushing out of the unemployment bathroom as if she just left a stinky load that she didn't want to leave at home.

Uh-oh.

When she came out into the waiting area, the office was empty and dark. She glanced around the room and looked up at a big analog clock above where the smug little receptionist sat. It was 12:10. *Shit!* The illuminated number on the waiting board that indicated the last number called was 82. *Shit, shit, shit!! I missed my turn! Ugh, now I'm going to have to start my wait time all over again.* She was pissed. Plus, she assumed that she was locked in and she knew that government workers always took extremely long breaks. Why not? It's just the taxpayers' money, right? She sat down in one of those horrible, vinyl chairs and put her head down in her hands and shook her head. *I'm hungry! Lazy ass government workers! Who takes an hour and a half lunch??* She got up out of the chair and began walking briskly – she had to confirm her suspicion. She was starving. She walked over and jostled the door. As she suspected, the door was locked. *Ugh!!* She was mad. As she prepared to put her head against the glass door, she sighed. She understood. Emotions aside, she knew that she had to be realistic; she simply wasn't going to get out of this horrible office until after lunch. She also realized that she probably wasn't going to be able to see an unemployment officer today and that means no benefits for at least a couple more weeks. Best case scenario is that they let her get back on the waiting list after lunch, in which case she was not going to eat for at least three or four more hours. *Shit, shit,*

shit!!! She wasn't sure what was worse – waiting another three hours to eat or being broke for a few more weeks. When her stomach was calling, it was hard not to listen!

I could've just waited for that photoshoot. She sighed. *Ugh.* She heard that this was the point in a tragedy of "acceptance" – she already went through "denial" and "anger"...now she was accepting of her fate and was simply going to make the most of it. Granted, it might be a bit of a stretch to call this a "tragedy," but dammit she was hungry! *That's tragic!!* She sighed again, left the front area. She walked to the back of the room and poured herself some more coffee. *This coffee has been here all morning. Ew. This shit is like bathwater.* Nonetheless, starving and bored (and still a little bit perturbed about nobody commenting on her dark photos), she took her coffee, sat back down and opened her phone again.

The coffee literally tasted like a raw potato. It was warm, but it smelled sort of dank, like a shirt that sat in the washer too long after a washing. And it tasted like it smelled – like a wet shirt mixed with potato flesh. But she drank it anyway – she hadn't been this hungry in a long time. She pulled her phone out of her pocket and put in her passcode. Then she opened up Instagram, Twitter and Facebook, in that order, and checked the responses to her dark picture that caused this whole hungry mess.

Nothing. Not one comment.

She was seething. But she was also having a "moment." She read about moments – especially from her Indian friends – they seemed to have this intuition when a learning situation was happening. They were deep and spiritual, and she was, too – it was buried inside of her. That's what this whole thing was about. Right now, she was learning something about her fans/friends. Perhaps she was also learning about herself as well. Maybe she's not quite as interesting as she thought she was. That's deep. That was uncomfortable. *Do they really just want to see me? I thought they loved me.* Maybe her fans/friends' interest in her was not quite as pure as it seemed. That thought troubled her. That sucked. She finished up her cup of potato coffee and leaned her head back and closed her eyes. *Damn, I think I drank a bit too much of that coffee. I don't want to get up to go pee. But I know I'll like it even less if I wake up from a good nap and have to go pee.*

She looked at the clock once more before she fell asleep – 12:23.

LISA

Lisa was, on the surface, the exact opposite of Delilah. She was born and raised on the Flathead Reservation in Montana in a small community called Elmo. She's left the reservation before – on many occasions – but has never lived anyplace else. As with most Kootenai people[5] on the Flathead reservation, most of her family lived immediately around her in Elmo. There were Kootenais elsewhere – Canada, Idaho, etc. – but if you were from Elmo, you tended to stay around Elmo. And why wouldn't you? It was a beautiful, spiritual and spooky place – glass-clear lake and gorgeous mountain views directly to the east, foothills directly to the west, and fresh air, huckleberries and love all around – but it was all she ever knew. She was born on the reservation, raised on the reservation, she worked on the reservation; she was an administrative assistant at the Tribe's administration office in Pablo.

Her life was here. Her ancestors were from here. She knew exactly where she came from.

She was also very much unlike Delilah because she's kept the same job for over twelve years. She just turned thirty a few months ago having immediately gone on the job market after graduation from high school. *Why go to college? I know what I want to do, I know who I want to serve and I know where I want to be.* She loved her job. She's had opportunities for advancement because she's smart, she works hard, and – once again, unlike Delilah – she's able to hide her social media habits from her supervisors. Still, every time she gets a

---

[5]The Flathead reservation is actually not one tribe, but several, hence the tribe's legal name is "Confederated Salish and Kootenai Tribes," which also includes the Pend d'Oreille people.

chance to move up the food chain at work, she politely declines. "I don't want more responsibility than I currently have. I'm happy with my job. Anyway, you won't pay me any better for doing more work."

Her white, university-educated supervisor would try to persuade her, "But Lisa, you're the most-qualified to move up the organizational chart. We need to get tribal members into these supervisory positions." Lisa's supervisor was a sweet woman who truly wanted to see tribal members in positions of authority. But more authority didn't tempt Lisa – she loved her freedom. She didn't want to have to carry around a Blackberry and feel chiefy. She knew that a Blackberry was actually a handcuff that meant that you didn't have an excuse not to return emails or pick up the phone immediately. *No, thank you. I'll just keep paying my own phone bill.*

Therefore, Lisa would reply, "But if all the most-qualified people just left to take over their own departments, there would only be less-qualified people helping you. And I want you to look good. Plus, if the Tribe really wanted to get tribal members to want to be in supervisory positions, they would offer us the same money as all of you non-tribal member supervisors get. I guess there'd be a lot more interest then."

The supervisor would concede her point. She had to. Lisa was right – the tribal members got paid less than the non-Native professionals that they brought in. Although she was very satisfied with her job and loved her coworkers, she wondered why that was the case. Sure, most places pay college grads and masters', etc, a bit more because of the education. But if all things were equal – the competency, the work product, the level of responsibility – did it matter whether it was a college grad who did the work or not? *It doesn't seem right.* Lisa wasn't going to raise a big stink about it – she enjoyed her job. But she just wasn't going to do just as good, if not better, at the same job as some white woman (or a white man) for less money. *No, thank you.*

Unless they threw a bunch of money at her, she only wanted to be responsible for herself.

That way she could get on Facebook (her favorite), Twitter and Instagram from her phone at work. She connected with people from all over the world. Of course, most of the people she connected with were other Indians (it was fun to talk about pow-wows and who's hooking up with who), but still she could connect with other people as well if she really wanted to. Once, she had a three-week internet romance with an Arab guy who had a bunch of tattoos. They both followed #HotAndBrown on Instagram and then she "liked" one particular picture that highlighted his shoulder tattoos. She started following him and then aggressively "liked" all of his photos. He liked her Instagram name, "IndigenousGoddessForYou," and so he posted the caption "Lovely New Friends ♥ ♥ ♥ ♥" with a screen capture photo of her liking all of his photos. In internet romance steps, that's almost equivalent to a promise ring and so he reciprocated by liking all of her photos. After making that decision, they exchanged cell phone numbers and texted each other and snap-chatted each other and even sent a couple of naughty pictures back and forth. After a few weeks, they seemingly simultaneously came to the realization that this handsome Arab man is probably never coming to Montana, and this cute Kootenai woman is probably never going to United Arab Emirates, and they sort of stopped communicating.

After her initial sadness at her social media relationship ending, she smiled and thought, *No pregnancies, no STDs – man was that fun.*

Unlike Delilah, Lisa never posted in reaction to her failed romances. She never put out cryptic Facebook statuses about how someone doesn't deserve her at her best if they cannot deal with her at her worst. She never posted sexy pictures of herself (Lisa was a very cute girl – not a spectacular beauty – with extremely long black hair, pouty lips and a round brown face) after a break-up to vie for attention from other men to make her feel better. Instead, she always maintained exactly the same profile picture – Lisa and her niece decked out in orange-ish fancy shawl outfits, posing at a pow-wow. Huge smiles. That was life in a nutshell: work, pow-wows, family.

And spirituality.

Delilah came from a so-called "traditional" Ktunaxa family. What that meant is that when the St. Ignatius Mission was established in 1854, Delilah's family was very vocal in their opposition to it. She remembered her grandpa saying, "Those are not our ways! We do not pray with the black robes!" Instead, the family moved north, away from the Mission and continued to practice the same spiritual practices they always did. She came from a long line of celebrated "seers" – people who saw things, spiritually, that other people did not. Indian people came from around the country and Canada to see her Grandpa – she remembered that. He was renowned. She went to the ceremonies and, although she never saw anything of a spiritual nature, honored that legacy. She attributed her lack of deep spiritual experiences to modern technology and stimulation – there just wasn't enough silence for her to see or hear what the spirits were telling her. She loved technology. She also loved her family's and people's traditions. However, when there was a conflict, there was no question. For example, Lisa refused to take "selfies" because their family still believed that photographs take a piece of your soul. Lisa didn't necessarily believe this herself, but she respected her family's belief enough that she wouldn't do it.

Lisa befriended Delilah because Delilah seemed to have a genuine interest in pow-wows and Native spirituality. And Lisa, like most Montana Indian girls, was raised on country music. When they first began chatting regularly, Lisa had a million questions for Delilah about Nashville and the Grand Ole Opry and Dwight Yoakam. She thought Dwight had the cutest butt in the whole wide world. Of course, Delilah hated country music and couldn't really her give adequate answers – but she faked it for the first couple of weeks *(thank God for Wikipedia!).*

Finally, she had to confess to Lisa, "Um, yeah, I live in Nashville but I never really got into the music. Not that I think it's bad…it's just not my favorite." Country music never came up again.

But they still had pow-wows and Indians. The way that they made each other's acquaintance was this: they both liked to look at pictures on Instagram under the hashtag #RealIndians. At first, Delilah would post all of those cheesy/creepy Native-themed memes with wolves and stars and strong Indian warriors on them.

Lisa would humorously comment that the Native men do not look like that where she comes from. It was funny, and cynical – but she always did it with good humor. Pretty soon, like the Arab man, Lisa and Delilah were communicating outside of social media. They were soon friends.

They would message each other on Facebook all day. Lisa was constantly telling Delilah about how reservation life really was and how the Indians she knew really were. She told her about the ceremonies that she went to and the stories about her family members seeing and hearing spirits.

Lisa was the one who told her about the spiritual value of mirrors. Once she told her, "You have to be careful with your looks, Delilah. You're always looking in the mirror, and the mirrors reflect spirits... there's nothing wrong with looking respectable and clean. But spirits get jealous – they're no longer here on this Earth, and they see you wasting all the time that you've been blessed with on this Earth staring in the mirror. They get jealous and impatient with that type of vanity. Sort of like that Greek story about that guy who turned into a flower. But the Indian version, AYEEZZZZZZ!!!" She always ended her lessons with humor. Still, Delilah could tell that she was serious.

Another time she typed, "You have to respect mirrors. They are not just for vanity and fixing your lipstick – they are medicine. I know you love looking at yourself in the mirror, LOL. But seriously, IJS...they can show you more than if your makeup is on right. LMAO. They can show you what you're doing right or wrong, girl. Look deeper into the mirror. Just don't bonk your head. ROFL." Lisa wasn't actually quite rolling on the floor, but Lisa had a very loud, deep laugh and she put it on full display when she typed that. Her officemates looked up from their Facebook conversations to see why she was laughing, smiled at her, and then quickly got back to their business.

Lisa had a big Indian girl laugh. She pointed when she laughed.

Delilah chuckled softly when she read Lisa's advice. *She's so silly.* Delilah was biologically Native, but she didn't laugh like an Indian girl. She had a girly, soft laugh. When Native women laugh, if a person listens closely enough they can hear centuries of heartache and pain, and so the laugh comes out that much more desperately. It was like eating a peanut butter and jelly sandwich after not eating for three days – yes, the sandwich is good on its own merits, but within the desperate context it's one of the most amazing things in the world!

And that's why Delilah loved hearing Lisa's laugh when they spoke on the phone. *She's earned that laugh. I've never had to work for my laugh – overlook poverty or alcoholism or abuse to find the humor. It's easy to laugh when everything's going right...when the fish are jumping and the cotton is high. Native people have the most beautiful laughs in the world because they found ways to laugh when everything was wrong.*

She loved to hear Lisa talk about the ceremonies that she grew up in and tried to imagine what they were like even though Delilah had never been to a ceremony. She had never been to a reservation either or even another Native person's house!! Lisa was her connection to all things Native, and so they stayed in contact every single day. Lisa's influence was profound – she sent Delilah some sweetgrass and kinnickkinnick and taught her how to pray. Delilah was sprung – she felt like she "belonged" in a way that she never had. Lisa warned her about how important it was to be solemn with these medicines. She told her how a person's thoughts and prayers are supposed to be for other people – *they're not for yourself. You gotta think of others and get over yourself.* Lisa told Delilah about how, in ceremony, if you are focused on self, the spirits will remind you where your mind and heart are supposed to be. Focused on others. Pray for others. Pray for the Earth. Pray for peace and understanding. Lisa said that she had a cousin who was always sulking and pouting and generally just worried about himself in ceremony; that cousin got done with a ceremony one time and "it looked like someone kicked the shit out of him," Lisa said. "Be careful," she warned her again.

She wrote a short note in the package that contained the sweetgrass and kinnickkinnick:

Delilah –
    These prayers and medicines are powerful, Delilah. We joke around a lot, but I want you to respect them. You must not be selfish or mix manipulation with the prayers you send with these. This isn't love medicine – don't wear it for perfume! LOL! Make sure, ok? Love ya!
                        Lees

Delilah was falling in love with Lisa. Not in a romantic or amorous sort of way, but she truly felt like she loved Lisa. Lisa looked out for her spiritual well-being; no one's ever done that before. They even planned to meet in person. Delilah had to – this lady was too powerful and too giving. She messaged Lisa, "If I can keep a job for longer than a month. LMFAO. I'm going to come see you this summer. Hopefully I can stay for a few weeks. I just need to find a boss who will keep me around. Maybe I need to show my boobs more. LOL."

Delilah wasn't laughing when she typed that. In fact, she wasn't even smiling. Instead, she was fighting back tears. She was sad because she realized that she knew someone on the other end of the computer who was pretty amazing and could teach her a lot about herself. *Things that I need to know.* But she couldn't afford to go and the reason why is because of her vanity and lack of discipline. *Why can't I be more like Lisa?* That was a funny question, because most people on Facebook who saw how close the two of them were figured that Lisa tagged along with Delilah because of Delilah's beauty. Many people figured that Delilah was the dominant figure in their relationship and that Lisa was merely supporting cast. They figured that she was the cute-yet-chubby friend of the hot girl who simply told the hot girl, "You go, girl" and took her leftovers.

But Delilah needed Lisa. Delilah knew it, too.

BABIES

The conversation moved across the messenger window at a breakneck speed.

> Girl, he is sexy.

Delilah attached a picture of the sexy man to her message. He really was sexy. He was built like Native men are built when they put aside the wheat products and sugar and work a job that requires manual labor. The Rock worked construction. Slim, small waist, big shoulders – he didn't have an ounce of body fat on him. Lisa had no choice but to agree with Delilah.

> Yeah he is, Dolly LOL. You sure he doesnt have kids?

Lisa liked to call Delilah "Dolly." She told her that her name sounds kinda like "Dolly" – that's why she called her that. Delilah liked to think that it was because she had big, voluptuous boobs and a tiny waist. She did have a tiny waist, but her boobs were decent-sized. Only a Hobbit would think that they were huge.

> He told me that he doesnt have any. I don't really believe him. I'm kinda playing with him – teasing him a little bit. I dont really think hes telling the truth because he kinda hesitated when I asked him. I was like 'I dont mind if you do.' He was like 'I really dont. I want to have kids though.' He said that he just got out of a LTR and that it was brutal, so hes going to be really careful getting into another LTR. He asked me if my real name is Giada. He said he liked Delilah better but I could tell that he wanted to call me Sexy Native Giada. I think he likes her smile – he said that he likes her cooking, but I think its her big ass smile.

> So hes on the rebound from Giada?
> She was too brutal for him? LOL

> Lisa, your terrible! LMAO Maybe he's on the rebound a little bit... But hes sexy and I've wanted to find a sexy Native man since like forever.

I know he likes the way I look. Im going to try to get him to fly down here – a fling. I know hes a player, so Im gonna play him.

SMH. SMDH, Delilah. –Sigh– Wheres he from?

He said hes from Standing Rock. Damm hes got some big ol sexy lips.

I'll just call him "The Rock" then. AYEZZZZ!!

LMAO!

I have my unemployment meeting in a few days. I have to go find some paperwork and check stubs for that. Text me later!

What day is your appointment?

The fifteenth – um, thats what, in two days? I'm gonna go look for this stuff, Lisa! TTYS!

I have to go too – boss is coming. I got to actually do some work – unlike you, you bum GAHHHHHH!!!! TTYL Dolly!

Delilah enjoyed her morning chats with Lisa. They centered her for the rest of the day. It didn't matter; whether she was at work or "on sabbatical" (on sabbatical has become her default response when people ask her why she isn't working), she needed to talk to Lisa. She told Lisa everything – when they first started communicating, Delilah loved dating white men. Delilah admitted, "I was raised as a white girl, Lisa. My dad – or the guy who I thought I was my dad – is white. Of course I'm going to date white men."

Now, since Lisa's become her best friend, she only wants to date Native men. "I need little Indian babies." She hadn't been a practicing Native even a year and she was already talking about Indian babies! Now, granted, she wasn't entirely convinced that she wanted babies at all – *they'll cut into my picture time.* Still, after a few months of going through all of her friends' Instagram accounts and she began to see what all the fuss was about. *They're beautiful.* Within a few months she was commenting about how Indian babies were the cutest babies on the planet – the chubby cheeks, spiky hair and fat bellies. She loved them and wanted one. *That would make me totally Native – to have a Native baby.*

She was now a convert.

She started having dreams about some of the pictures she saw – little babies in moccasins. Babies in pow-wow regalia. She wondered if she was Kootenai like Lisa. Or maybe she was a Lakota woman like Mary Crow Dog; she loved the book, "Lakota Woman," and loved the idea of coming from that sort of noble lineage. She was pretty sure that she wasn't Hopi or Zuni – she heard that they were really short people, and she wasn't.

Her adoptive parents never, ever talked about her birth parents. They told her that her biological parents made them promise they would never tell her anything other than that they loved her. The only facts that they would divulge is that they adopted her ("God blessed us with you – handed you to us like He handed Bithiah baby Moses in the river...praise Him....") when she was three months old and that she came from a very poor, very tough place. She asked questions – ever since she was a little girl, she always asked them where her birth family was from and whether or not her birth mother was beautiful. They never told her – all her adoptive parents said was that they really knew nothing about her birth parents other than that they wanted a better life for her. But her adoptive parents said that even if they did know where the biological parents were from, they made them promise that they wouldn't tell her anything – that was actually one of the terms of the adoption. Legal terms – it was written into the adoption documents. Her adopted dad told her, "Their life was very difficult where they were from. They didn't want you to ever go there – they didn't want you to have to see the pain that they saw or experience the frustration and hopelessness that they saw. They wanted to give you real opportunity."

She believed them. They wouldn't lie. Plus, she couldn't think of an upbringing that would give her more opportunities.

She was raised in a wealthy community called Old Hickory. If that isn't the oldest and whitest sounding suburb in the world, I don't know what is. But she wasn't bitter about her upbringing – how could she be? She was a child of privilege. She went to one of the best schools in the state of Tennessee, she had a very nice car at sixteen, a Honda Accord. She was raised as the only child, the apple of her parents' eyes – they loved their little brown baby, their "sweet little Pocahontas" – and were cognizant of her biological family's dire straits. Thus, they made sure that she didn't experience any of the difficulty that her biological family did. All through school, she dressed like a Macy's model. She had a Shetland pony at their summer home (they would've bought her a unicorn or a liger if they could've). She had the chance to go to any college in the nation on their dime. She knew that she wouldn't have gotten those opportunities on the rez.

As much as she loved to romanticize life on the reservation, as much as she tried to identify with the beautiful struggle of being Indigenous in this country...as much as she did all of that, she had to be honest with herself. She simply would not have gotten all the opportunities that she had if she had grown up on the reservation. Even this current self-imposed poverty – she could go to her adopted parents and ask for a loan or tell them that she wanted to go back to school. How many Natives had the opportunity to do that?

She was raised with every opportunity in the world except the opportunity to know what it meant to be Native.

Now, she was taking that opportunity. Lisa was the guide to her new Native neighborhood, like the friendly lady across the street who catches you up on all of the local gossip. Lisa was her quick and dirty introduction into Indian Country – she learned the rest from social networking. Lisa told her that she would know when it was the right time – her Indian spirit would be breathed back into her, if she gave it a chance. Her next step was to physically get out and touch the earth in those places: Elmo, Porcupine, Eagle Butte, all the places that she's read about and imagines her soul calling home.

She couldn't wait. *Indian babies.*

FUTILITY

Lisa tried like hell to get hold of Delilah that day.

She found out some incredible news about The Rock. Giddy like a little girl, she couldn't wait to tell Delilah the newest gossip. This was undoubtedly good news – it wasn't as if she was telling Delilah that he had twelve kids by thirteen different women like many of the good-looking guys in Indian Country. No, she found out that he really didn't have any kids.

He wanted to have kids, though.

Lisa found out that he was on the rebound, that he got his heart broken by his ex-girlfriend. In fact, The Rock's ex-girlfriend was from just up the road on the Flathead Rez and used to attend Salish Kootenai College. They met online; she was a minor internet celebrity who fancied herself a model. She was very pretty, but she never got paid for any of her gigs. Nonetheless, her status made her an object of widespread adoration by men nationwide. They met at the Arlee pow-wow and hooked up. After their pow-wow romance ended, he would come to see her every other weekend. It was a beautiful Native romance – separated by hundreds of miles, yet with lust and a desire for beautiful brown Native babies overcoming that separation.

The young lady quickly got pregnant while they were together; The Rock (his real name was Leon) was happy about the pregnancy and actually moved out to Pablo to be closer to the young lady and her family. The Rock's mom wanted him to be a little more cautious. "Do you really know her, son?" His mom loved the idea of Native romance – she herself was romanced into coming to the Standing Rock reservation by Leon's dad. She was Navajo, from New Mexico, and moved up after they were married. No, she wasn't against the idea of a torrid romance that took her son to the beautiful Flathead Reservation at all. But she wasn't crazy about the girl. When The Rock showed his mom her pictures on her Facebook page, she said, "Yeah, she sure is beautiful." But then when she continued to look at her page, she felt compelled to ask, "Why does she take so many pictures of herself?"

The Rock explained to her that she's a model, and models are always in front of the camera. The Rock's mom retorted with, "I thought the deal with models was that they had other people take pictures of them?" The Rock's mom also didn't like the fact that so many men seemed to take an interest in her. "Does she have to show so much of her body? Do you really want that many men knowing what your woman looks like almost buck-naked?" The Rock was comfortable with it. He knew that came with the territory – beautiful women had adoring fans. His mom, in the end, was supportive. "Son, I just want you to be careful. When someone takes that many pictures of themselves and spends that much time in front of the mirror, it's gonna be hard for them to love you as much as they love themselves. It's called "vanity," son. I don't think vanity is good for a relationship. The ancestors don't like vanity – a mother's focus is supposed to be on the development of the baby and the family and the inside, not the outside. Beauty fades, and how she's going to feel after that beauty's gone?"

She was just looking out for her son. She was a good mother. She would be an amazing grandmother.

And just like the good Native mother/grandmother she is, she was right there when it was time came for the baby to be born. In fact, his whole family – literally about eighteen of them – drove in from Standing Rock to greet the beautiful, spiky-haired Native baby. When the baby was born, however, it had blonde hair – "that's not unusual," the new paternal grandmother said. "We have some Irish in our family." But the family began to wonder a bit when the baby was about a month old because the baby literally had the smallest little lips they ever seen and the baby's hair never changed colors. It was still blonde. After a few more months – when the baby was about five months old – The Rock's mother told him, "Son, I want you to find out if that baby boy is really yours. I don't know...." When she said "I don't know," that meant "I know." The Rock didn't want to get a DNA test at first. He didn't want to find out because he kind of knew, too. But finally, at the prodding of his mom, he finally got a test done over the Flathead girl's protests.

The baby wasn't his. Evidently she had a thing for big, farmer-type German white boys, and this baby should've been dressed in baby-sized lederhosen and not Standing Rock-style moccasins.

Obviously this was bad news for The Rock and his family. It was a sad situation, and Lisa didn't take any joy in the fact that he had to go through this. *He sounds like a really nice guy.* It was, however, very good news for Delilah. *But she can't be playing with this boy. He's delicate....*

Lisa got into work about 8:45. She called – everything went straight to voicemail. That wasn't unusual; Lisa knew that Delilah was at home and her apartment had absolutely terrible service. Lisa lived pretty far out on the rez, in Elmo, and so her reception at her house was pretty bad, too. She couldn't really use Instagram in Elmo. She only did Instagram on her phone, not on her computer. She thought anybody who did Instagram on their computers were weirdos. But that's the rez – you kind of expected bad reception there. *We're hunter-gatherers. We don't use technology,* Lisa chuckled at the thought. But she expected more in a major metropolitan area like Nashville. *It should at least be like it is in Missoula. In Missoula, the reception is much better than on the rez.* But Delilah's reception was horrible at home. Sometimes, in the middle of their nightly conversation, Delilah would start going in and out and Lisa would just get frustrated and say, "Girl, just text me."

She loved Delilah's southern accent ("Who knew that Indian girls could talk like Dolly Parton?"). But she hated not being to hold a complete conversation because of the constant fading in and out, in and out. So Lisa knew that it had to be that Delilah just didn't get her calls. Next, she started texting. No response. She left six Facebook messages ("Call me!"), without even checking her Facebook activity. She just couldn't wait to tell Delilah this news – her own stuff could wait. She also left three tweets. She double-checked her calendars, *yep, today's the fifteenth. She's supposed to be at the unemployment office all day. Sometimes those buildings get no reception.* She figured that she would leave a message on her Instagram, just in case. She knew that Delilah liked to check that the most – *that girl loves putting up pictures of herself.*

But Lisa had to run some errands first. *Damn job gets in the way of my social life.* She had a decent social life. The truth is that Lisa loved the ladies in the administration building. Someone was always cooking or having a birthday or retiring or something. Very close-knit group. She'd bring candy and leave it on her desk; she knew which candy everyone in the office liked. She was happy at home, but she loved to expand her horizons and learn about people around the country, too (and even in the Middle East!). Right now, before chasing this wild girl Delilah around Instagram, she had to go make some copies and make sure that the planning was done for a conference that her department was hosting. *I'm already a supervisor. Sheesh, I should get paid for that already.* She wasn't bitter – she actually took a great deal of pride in the amount of responsibility that her department entrusted her with. But days like this, she just wanted to give Delilah the scoop and she couldn't do that when she had to pay attention to silly little details like how many doughnuts the conference needs. She left her cell phone on her desk so she wouldn't be tempted to bug Delilah for a little while.

She was very aware of the time.

10:00 a.m. It was 11:00 a.m. in Nashville. *She's at her appointment. No need to bother her while she's in her appointment trying to get unemployment.* Lisa didn't know that Delilah came from wealthy people. She knew that she was adopted, and that she was raised by white people, but she didn't know that they were wealthy. She just knew that Delilah was struggling, broke – that's what Delilah told her. And it was the truth! Delilah really was broke, but she had a pretty good safety net. Still, the last thing Lisa wanted to do was distract Delilah when she was supposed to be getting some money from unemployment. She needs money. *Ok, I'll wait.*

Lisa's errands kept her busy until lunchtime – one o'clock Nashville time. She figured that Delilah was probably getting home from some lunch and getting ready to hop online. Lisa was bursting at the seams to tell her the story – they hadn't communicated at all this morning. She was finally going to get her Delilah fix and tell her to call her. Lisa began loading up her Instagram because she couldn't seem to get hold of her via text or phone calls. She started loading up Delilah's account – it was taking a little while. *Slow connection on the rez today.* She typed in "Lovely Native Giada." *Oh look, this girl is already posting pictures of herself this morning. Can't return a text, but can post pictures of herself. What am I going to do with her?* Lisa knew that Delilah was doing these more abstract, more honest, depressed photos in the morning – she "didn't want to show more of herself." *She wants her followers to like her for her inside beauty now.* Lisa was sarcastic about it, but she truly believed in Delilah's internal beauty – she knew that she was a beautiful girl. But she was also realistic – *she started off by showing these horny ass Indian boys her boobs and legs. Of course that's what they want to see now. Kinda hard to unfry that bread.*

Lisa went directly to Delilah's page – this morning she didn't really want to scroll through the entire list of hoochies and memes and pictures of guys smoking weed. Usually she enjoyed it – she had a lot of muscle-bound guys on the list of people that she followed, and she enjoyed looking at them. But not today. She had bidness to attend to! She used the "explore" option and typed in "Lovely Na...." That's all she needed to type and the app's auto-finish filled in the rest; Delilah's name came up. She clicked on the first picture, the newest one; she planned to comment on every single one of her photos until she responded, from the newest to the oldest.

There was one of Delilah's "dark" photos (Lisa called them her "deep" photos) – in the mirror. According to Instagram, it was taken one hour (1h) ago. She looked, and there were no likes and no comments. *That is so weird. Men comment on every single photo that she posts.* She usually didn't comment on these because she just didn't "get" them – she thought that they were kind of silly. Delilah was undoubtedly Lisa's BCF – her Best Cyber Friend – and so it wasn't like she didn't comment regularly on her photos. In fact, Lisa was always the first to comment on pretty much anything she posted and say some supportive or complimentary things about Delilah because she knew Delilah better than most. But she just didn't "get" these.

But she had to comment on this one. She needed her morning dose (and to let her know this juicy bit of information about The Rock).

The picture began moving. That's not an altogether strange phenomenon. Although Instagram is a photo application that is intended to edit and/or post photos, recent upgrades also make it possible to post videos. However, when a person posts a video, a little video camera shows up on the upper right hand corner of the image. There was none here in Delilah's photo, but it started moving. It was pitch black in the room – still, the pitch black photo began to move.

Lisa could see a flash of light in the moving photo – it didn't look like a camera flash, but like lightning in a straight line. Concentrated flash. Lisa got a knot in her stomach – *what the hell is going on?* She clearly saw Delilah in typical "selfie" pose mode. But she was topless. Lisa muttered, very quietly, "What the fu...?? What are you thinking?" She could see the industrial paper towel dispenser and bathroom stalls; she could plainly see that this wasn't Delilah's bathroom (although she had never been to Delilah's place before, she was used to seeing her bathroom in her many bathroom selfies). This was someplace that looked industrial or corporate – probably the unemployment office. Within the next two seconds of looking at the moving photo, Lisa saw the concentrated flash split into two distinct figures. Those figures were no longer as bright as a flash – now they were vaguely orange and luminescent, like an ember, still hot after a raging fire. But there were distinctly two figures.

One of the orange-tinted figures moved toward the door. It stood in front of the door, holding the deadbolt as if it were trying to keep her locked in. The other figure stood directly on the right side of her (it was actually the left side, but it was in the mirror) and had a hand spread out over Delilah's face – you could still see her face because the hand was transparent, but that space was orange. The other hand looked to be in the small of Delilah's back. This figure was moving its hand slowly over Delilah's face, and staying right beside her as she looked around to see where the flash came from. The movement in the photo stopped there.

It now looked like a still shot – it was back to being a black photo. Lisa actually said, out loud, "Holy shit!" Her co-workers looked over at her inquisitively. Lisa knew that she was getting attention. She knew that she really didn't want to explain what she was cursing about, so she consciously muffled her reaction. After all, she wasn't sure whether what she saw was real or not. *They're gonna think I'm crazy.*

She looked at the photo again. This time, it was simply a still photo of blackness. She rubbed her eyes – same. She scrolled further down. There was another one of Delilah's photos. About an hour earlier.

The earlier photo was at Delilah's house, in her home bathroom. It wasn't as dark as the other photo – there was a faint light in the background. Lisa could see smoke drifting into the photo. *Is she a smoker? I didn't know that.* She glanced up, to see where her co-workers were, and when she glanced back at the photo the smoke was drifting upwards. Moving again. She had to verify that she wasn't crazy. *Someone else has to see this...*"VIVIENNE!!! VIVIENNE!!" Lisa called her co-worker over to check this out...the smoke didn't stop moving; she had to make sure that her co-worker saw it, too. "Do you see that, Viv??"

Vivienne ducked her head to be able to see the phone screen. "Oh my god – is that a video?? That's scary!"

"That is NOT a video, Viv. That's a picture that moves! What the hell???"

Vivienne began sniffing-there was a very apparent, foreign smell in the air. "Do you smell that?" her co-worker asked.

Lisa's eyes got huge. *What the hell is going on? Why is this fucking phone smelling like this?* A chill ran up her spine and she got butterflies in her stomach; Lisa knew exactly what that smell was. "Fuck...she's burning medicine while taking these pictures!"

Her co-worker didn't see the gravity of the situation. She figured it was a new app or something, and was more concerned about the smell and being nosy than how it was happening. "Who is that?"

Lisa didn't have an opportunity to respond. As the smell of sweetgrass and kinnickkinnick rose from the phone and filled the entire office, the image on the phone's screen grew more aggressive. They saw the same orange figures that Lisa saw earlier enter the bathroom behind her silhouette. "What the hell is that?? What the hell is going on, Lees??" her co-worker demanded.

Lisa didn't answer – she pressed the square button at the bottom of her phone and closed out Instagram. She didn't explain to her co-worker, instead she began dialing Delilah's number. *Answer, answer, answer!!!! She called again and again. Please answer, D....*

Nothing.

THE ROCK

He was heartbroken. Embarrassed. He tried to pretend that he knew. He didn't know. He had no clue. He wanted to believe her. *Mom knew. Mom always knows. She always told me that the beautiful ones are the most insecure ones. They're the ones who need the most attention. She was right.*

"Leon. Leon. Baby, turn off your lights. Take your jeans off." His mom woke him, as she used to do when he was a little kid. Since he moved back to Standing Rock, he'd been living with her again. He needed her. Again.

He fell asleep with his lamp on. He was writing. Since he found out the baby wasn't his, he'd been writing more and more and talking less and less. He told his mom that he writes poetry – what Leon didn't tell her was that he also wrote love notes to his supposed-to-be baby's mama. He wrote to her and told her that he wanted her back – that there was a piece of him missing. Two pieces, actually – her and the baby. He didn't care that the baby was someone else's; people make mistakes and he was willing to raise someone else's baby.

Even if that baby didn't look like him.

He always wanted beautiful Indian babies – long black hair, brown skin. He told her in the letters that they could have thirty babies that looked like that. They just needed to start over, maybe move away, where nobody knew who they were and nobody knew their story. Someplace where people wouldn't judge. *Indian people are so judgmental. I know her friends would be laughing at me if they saw me every single day. They're just little girls – they don't understand that love is about pain and forgiveness. It's not just about love songs and matching shoes. I forgive you. I'd forgive you a million times if you'd just pretend that nothing ever happened and come back to me. I know you'd feel guilty and probably wouldn't forgive yourself, but I forgive you, baby.*

He never sent the letters or the poems to her. He couldn't. His pride wouldn't let him. He burned them in the same giant abalone shell that he burned his sweetgrass and sage. He offered them up as prayers to the Creator. He prayed out loud, "Please take this hurt in my heart away. I never ask for anything – I don't believe in asking you, who has given me so many gifts, for anything. But I'm asking for this. There is a hole in me, like I've drunk gallons of bleach, Creator. And it hurts my stomach and heart. Please take the hurt away."

He burned the poems. But before he did, he would say them aloud. He called this one, "How to Say I Love You in Indian."

HOW TO SAY I LOVE YOU IN INDIAN
In Three Parts

I

We asked for hands in marriage
With horses and by chopping wood for grandmas
By providing prospective moms and dads with dry meat aplenty
Fish by the dozens
Buffalo robes by the twenty
Staying warm was valued over a ring that is coveted by many
No need for diamonds
A bunch of seal grease and deer meat are an Indigenous girl's best friends
Cockles, clams and salmon with some peppermint tea at the end.
"Don't tell me how you'll take care of my daughter
Show me."

II

No one can get lied to like a Native
It's in our blood like crying or fighting when we're drunk
*From **"We come in peace"***
*To **"Your handsome little boy is safe with our priest."***
Our faith is our strongest strength and our weakest weakness
All at the same time.
We have very little value for words
Linguists wonder why our languages aren't written.
The answer: written words ain't shit
We learned that from America and Great Britain
And France and Spain
Charlatans with beautiful written languages
Made promises they never intended to keep
Why would we trust mere words again?
We learned why white people say that "talk is cheap."
We just wish you would have told us a little bit earlier.
Words mean something to Natives.
Still
We had to learn the game
Devalue words
Like American currency
Promise ourselves: "never again."
Because no one can get lied to like a Native.
We go against spiritual natures now
Although inherently creatures of faith
Now questioning everything
Enduring images of ancestral wraiths
*"Don't believe it. Don't believe it. Don't believe it. **By God,** whatever*
you do, don't believe it."
We are a beautifully flawed race of untrusting people
Expectation of disappointment and scars of betrayal litters the tissue
around our hearts
Abandonment issues and fear of failure ever-present
Self-sabotage before we get a chance to play the fool.

III

He was smitten
An Indian boy
Not raised around Indian people
But as an adult wanted to find a Native wife.
He thought he found the one
Tried to convince her that he was different
Wrote her letters and poems declaring his devotion
Romantic Indian boy courting a cute Indian girl
A single mom
Discouraged by her lack of emotion
Asked her beautiful brown son if it was ok if he gave him a brother
The boy would smile at the suitor
He knew that the man was good for his mother
Still she was unwilling to accept his words
He'd make promises
Tell her that he wanted to take care of her
She put her fingers to his lips as if to say "shush."
Tell him "Hush your little white lies
Charming little white boy
We have the rest of our lives
What's the rush?"
She rebuffed him for six months
He thought she was perfect but he finally had enough
He was convinced she didn't want to be his
"I'm not Indian enough"
He was in tears and ready to give up
Writing a "Dear Jane" letter taking breaks from packing his stuff
And she walked in.
She was crushed
"Where are you going?"
"It's obvious you don't love me."
"I'm here aren't I? I haven't left.
You just don't speak Indian.
Stop saying you love me
That means less than nothing
Speak in my language
We can give it a real try.

If you really want to stay together we've got to pray together
Indians don't do this in-law shit
My family is your family all the way together
For better or for worse
All of us hang out every Saturday together
Also.
You and my son need to play together.
Without me.
You will have to get comfortable with disciplining him
All the way up to whooping that ass
Patiently take him fishing and proudly take him to class
He's going to look up to you
You've got to be beyond reproach
I expect you to WANT to think through your every step
Premeditate your whole life's approach
You'll be a daddy.
I don't need another absentee baby's daddy
Who's only there when it's convenient
Too many Indian kids suffer from love that's too convenient
Being a dad ain't convenient. A child ain't convenient. Being together
ain't convenient. Staying together ain't convenient.
I want you to say you love me with your suffering. With your patience.
With your pain. With your resilience and forgiveness. With your time.
With your sacrifice.

Anything but with your words.

Qunukumken
Txin Yaktakuq
Sil n'zhoo
Biixoo3é3e
Nimitzlaco 'tla
KitAKOMIMMO
Nemusa Iswa
Ee'hitewisa
Gv-ge-yu-hi
Ne mehotatse
Chiholloli
Chi hullo li

U kamakutu nu
Kwin-ca-minch
Kisakihitin
Aloha wau ia oe
Nu' umi unangwa'ta
Aakuluk
Iiteéminó
Aim go-doe bee-el-doe
Moo ams ni stinta
Ne-stl' i Nexw
Ketapanen
Nowehkowai
Konorónkhwa
Ayoo aniinish'ni
Kana misk hitjup
Ku'nolhkwa
Gunowe'nkhwa
Gazahagin
Gzaagin
Tu uste yoom
KtabanIn
Ketebanene
Yunowmoie
Ayor anosh'ni
Neh ume chasuequanda
Techihhila
Enyi sum'oh hoyt
Atowweeshmash
Atawishamash
'Enk'ay sih
Dom ho' ichema
yaOOkOOksOOwha

Five minutes later the poem went up in flames in the abalone shell.

MEDICINE

12:30.

Damn, I'm freezing!! I gotta go pee!! Delilah shivered and then opened her eyes. She looked around to see if anybody saw her shivering. Of course there was nobody else in the unemployment office – it was still lunch time – but looking around guiltily just seemed like a habit when she fell asleep in a public place. She held her crotch, too lazy to get up to go to the bathroom. *I wanna go back to sleep!!* It felt like she had been sleeping for hours, but when she woke up, it showed that only slept for twelve minutes. Her dreams were intense – she wondered how she had dreams so quickly if she only went to sleep for twelve minutes? She dreamed that there were a whole bunch of strangers watching her as she danced naked. Not as a stripper – she was doing some artistic dance, and it looked beautiful. Nonetheless, despite the beauty of the dance and the artistry of the situation, she felt like she should have been clothed. Being naked made her feel ashamed. And cold. The cold made her have to go pee.

She was still tired. But her bladder was calling.

She begrudgingly got out of her seat. She was angry, disgusted at the coffee that she had earlier. It was like a bad sexual experience – a double whammy. After a bad sexual experience she would always feel horrible because she would realize that 1) not only did she not get off, but also 2) now she has to worry about this creep with six-minute stamina and bacne (back acne) calling her and wanting to be her boyfriend. Similarly, here she not only 1) had a horrible taste in her mouth that tasted like she drank coffee after brushing her teeth with instant potato flakes, but also 2) now it messed up her wonderful little nap. *Fuck.*

She quickly walked toward the bathroom not quite doing the bathroom dance. *I still have another hour to go.* She opened the bathroom door; the light was still on. She darted toward the stall. "Ahhhhhhhhhhhhhhhhh..." *That was freaking amazing.* She pulled her phone back out of her pocket and began going through her various social media. *Nothing, nothing, nothing. Not a single comment* from her earlier photo shoot. *Freakin' cowards! Can't deal with a real woman, a spiritual woman.* She was mad that The Rock didn't comment. *He's just as shallow as the rest. He only wants me for my beauty – nasty, he's probably got a bunch of kids all over the place and diseases. Thinks he's all that. Fucker.*

She was angry. She decided, *Fuck this deep shit. They wanna only see me sexy, that's cool. I'm gonna give them a show.*

She wiped off her moisture and got off the john. She got out of the stall and washed her hands. She leaned over the counter facing the mirror so that she could see down her shirt. *Take that, fucking Rock. You will never see these pretty titties again.* She formed her lips into the prettiest, most seductive pouty lips that she could, with her mouth slightly open. She was looking seductive. *Fierce.* No lights off this time – *I want you to see this and miss what you could have had.* With her left hand, she pulled her shirt down a little bit more so that you could see more of her breasts; with her right hand, she held the phone down by the counter with the camera "on" so that she could snap it at the perfect moment. *This is going to be my new profile picture. All of these guys will be on me after this.*

>click<

Just like earlier in the day, lights flashed before her eyes, as if the camera phone's flash was super-powered. It knocked her off-balance, she lost her equilibrium and began to feel lightheaded. Delilah fell backwards to the linoleum floor and took one last look up at the fluorescent lights above before she closed her eyes. She dreamed about the color orange.

DESSERTS

Lisa hadn't spoken to Delilah in several days. She wasn't sure what to think. She was pretty sure that something bad happened to her – why else wouldn't she hear from her? There was no other reason that those pictures were moving, or why those images appeared behind her. She knew that they weren't good signs. Lisa had heard about spirits all her life – she was aware they were there even if she never saw them herself. She knew that Delilah had somehow offended those spirits. Lisa never saw anything of a supernatural nature before that moment – she heard a million stories about supernatural events and visions (bears coming into sweatlodges, buffalos talking to people), but never saw them. Who would believe that her first experience or vision would come in a smartphone?? Yet, she knew that what she saw was powerful and real. And dangerous.

Lisa had called 911 to tell them that something was wrong in some unemployment office in Nashville. She didn't know the address of the unemployment office. The only information she had was Delilah's name and her phone number, which she gave to the dispatcher. But she didn't know if it was in the city of Nashville proper, or whether it was in some suburb. 911 didn't really help – they said to call back if she got more information. She didn't call 911 anymore. She didn't know any of Delilah's family members, so she couldn't call them. She did Facebook message a few mutual friends to see if anyone heard from her. No one had. She called a bunch that same day. She texted a bunch that day, too. She followed up for about a week, because if something really bad did happen to her, there would be some record of it. *People don't just disappear, do they??* After a few weeks, she didn't call anymore. She didn't text anymore. She knew that if she was missing or killed, the authorities would go through her texts and phone calls and Facebook messages to see who contacted her. Lisa didn't want to look like a stalker or some crazy person who might've killed her. Plus, she didn't want those spirits to follow her. She would certainly be there if Delilah called, but she wasn't going to invite those spirits into her life. That's white people shit. *If the spirits want Delilah, they're going to take Delilah. I'm not strong enough to change their minds. I'll pray for her and make offerings for her. But I cannot save her.*

She checked Delilah's Facebook and Twitter and Instagram for some sign that she was ok. There was nothing. Lisa kept checking them – no updates, no new pictures, no new comments. Nothing. Her accounts were gone.

SMILES

Almost a year to the day later, right at the beginning of October of the next year, Delilah finally contacted Lisa. By text. She'd deleted her Instagram, Twitter and Facebook months ago.

> Lees, I'm sorry I've been out of contact.
> Things changed. I hope you are well.

Lisa was very excited when she received the text and texted back within seconds.

> Girl, are you ok?? I thought you were dead. I couldn't get a hold of you. I need to talk to you. It's very, very important!

Lisa immediately dialed Delilah's number but the call went to voicemail.

Delilah texted her again.

> We'll talk soon. But not about that. I think I know what you're going to talk to me about. There's nothing to talk about. Ever. I'm ok. I'll get better. In either event, I can't worry about it right now. You know what I'm talking about. I'm happier and I understand. It was terrible and at the time I thought it was the end of my life, but it makes sense to me now. I'm actually kinda glad that it happened. LOL, I've had a job for six months straight now. It's a good job. I've also got a boyfriend.

> WTH are you talking about? What's "that?" What makes sense? I'm glad to hear about your job and your boy-friend, but you need to quit being so damn cryptic girl!! I'm glad you found a boyfriend...The Rock was taken off the market while you were MIA. Some sane lady finally decided to treat that boy nice...there's pictures of him and his old lady with the most beautiful Indian baby you've ever seen all over Facebook.

Delilah typed back.

> I'm glad. He sounded like a good guy. I wasn't ready for him at that time in my life, Lees. I would've messed it up. I'm glad, but as you know, I haven't been on Facebook in forever."

Answer my questions.
What's "that?" Why are you being so sneaky? What makes sense? Enough about the Rock. Both of you guys have somebody now. What the hell is going on, Delilah?

The stroke makes sense. My face makes sense. At first I was upset, resentful. Blamed God. I was angry. My doctor says that I was carrying a lot of stress because of unemployment, because of depression and abandonment. Because of money reasons. They said that the stress culminated with me not getting any nutrition that day of my appointment. They said it was a weird set of circumstances that made me have a stroke at such a young age. But you and I both know that it wasn't because of that. We don't have to tell them that and we don't need them to tell us that. We know what it was.

WTF???
STROKE???
Are you serious???
WTF???
You're way too young to have a stroke!!

Lees, it's ok. It's ok. You know what it was. I do too. I'm in a different place now. I was angry at first. But you tried to warn me. They're calling it a stroke. We both know what it was though. It's ok – it's not your fault. You tried to save me from it. Thank you. You did save me. The ambulance lady told me that some crazy lady called from Montana and told her that there was an emergency at an unemployment office. They said that they checked on a hunch – and a fire station was just right down the street from my unemployment office. You saved me from being fully paralyzed. Now, I'm able to work through it instead. They say that I can recover a lot with facial exercises and changing my diet. I think that'll help, but I know that prayers are important, too. Either way, I'm not too worried about it. I met this Choctaw guy from Mississippi. There's a lot of Choctaws here. He's the guy I've been seeing for the past few months. He doesn't mind – he saw my old pictures and told me that he would've been scared and intimidated to talk to me before. He says that likes me exactly the way I am.

Delilah sent one more text to reaffirm to Lisa.

It's ok, Lees.

Lisa didn't know what to say. She didn't respond anymore. She knew exactly what happened. She knew what it was. She sat at work and cried. Her beautiful friend.

She received one more text from Delilah, a picture mail. It was a picture of Delilah, with no text. She didn't have any makeup on and it didn't have any hashtags. She wasn't showing any cleavage and looked like she was about ten pounds heavier than the last time she saw her pictures. She looked beautiful – brown skin, almond eyes looking more gorgeous than ever, even though one eye was barely open.

The left half of her face was sagging badly. But she was finally smiling, not looking fierce at all.

(Thank you to Levi Rickert and the Native News Network for the list of translations of "I love you" in Native languages and to Frank Burns for adding to that list). www.nativenewsnetwork.com

THANK YOU, LYDIA
(A True Story)[6]

ACT 1
GODDESS

I'll call her "Lydia."

She changed my life pretty much as my life was just starting.

We were elementary school classmates in a small reservation town – the reservation was pretty damn big, but the town was tiny. The official population count of the town is a whisker over 1,000. It's safe to say that the population of the various communities around the town eclipsed that number by at least another five or six thousand Natives.

Like many people – Native and non-Native – who come from rural communities in Montana, we were fairly suspicious of the government and thus aren't the most apt to answer a census. Still, even not knowing exactly how many people lived there, it was safe to say that it wasn't a whole bunch. It was the type of town in which you maintain pretty much the same cadre of classmates from K-12, with few changes. Basketball, cheer squad, drama, all generally recycle the same cast of characters.

Our schools were like a brown-skinned version of Saved by the Bell. With long, beautiful, black braids. (I typically played the part of Screech because I have curly hair, am awkward and had a horribly shrill, pre-pubescent voice.) Our version of Saved by the Bell also featured kids wearing shoes from Volume Shoe Source and not Foot Locker.

Oh yeah, the kids were also resoundingly poor.

---

[6]A version of this story appeared in gawker.com's True Stories section, Kiese Laymon, Contributing Editor.

See, like most Indian reservations on the Great Plains, our reservation was genetically engineered to be economically poor.[7] Specific government policies that fundamentally destroyed Indigenous economies (as General Sheridan said, "Let them kill, skin, and sell until the buffalo is exterminated, as it is the only way to bring lasting peace and allow civilization to advance.") combined with utterly remote geography (barely a million people in the whole state of Montana currently, two hours from a city of 50,000 people), and a general lack of investment, created a place that has effectively maintained 70% unemployment for decades. It's one of those places where, many times, tribal members have to ostensibly make a decision, "I'm either going to struggle financially or I'm going to leave."

Some manage to make a very good living and stay home at the same time. Yet, it is difficult.

Still, the star of this story is not Poverty – it's lovely Lydia. Yes, it's absolutely important to contextualize that Poverty is a recurring and obnoxious character on our reservations, like Kramer on Seinfeld. We really don't like him, but we have to acknowledge him and try to our best to avoid paying too much attention to him. But like Kramer on Seinfeld, this story's not about Poverty – there are other characters who are much more interesting and do a much better job of telling the complete story. He's just a piece of the story. A bit player.

Plus, Poverty tends to show up everyplace; poor people pocketbooks and predicaments create poor people issues. It could

---

[7] Like many rural, isolated reservations, the lack of economic development on my reservation used to mean – as a general rule – that the cultural resources were/are very strong and robust. Typically reservations that are close to major metropolitan areas are the reservations with stronger economies. The flipside to that close proximity, however, is that those reservations and Native people oftentimes take on many of the characteristics, social problems and values of those major metropolitan areas. As children we simply could not be MTV kids because there was no cable where we lived and we were so far, geographically, away from mainstream radio stations/shopping/television stations. Therefore, those influences were largely kept away from us and we kind of had to focus on cultural things – from sports to pow-wow dancing to riding horses to ceremony. It was a bit easier to focus on those things because there weren't so many shiny things begging for your attention. Now, even on remote reservations, the internet has changed that focus substantially, with kids now having virtual/visual access to places that they've never been and developing many of the attributes of the rest of mainstream America.

be Black kids on Chicago's South Side or El Salvadoran youth in East Los Angeles or even White teens in Appalachia – poor people are poor people are poor people, and the issues within all of our poor communities are generally the same. "Untapped potential, limitless talent, but no institutional knowledge of how to succeed." Our reservation gives a case study into what those poor people issues look like among Native people.

But that's enough about Poverty's bitch ass. Let's get back to beautiful Lydia. The portrait of little Indian girl beauty. PLUS, she was vicious on the kickball field and could fancy dance like none other.

The complete package.

I remember we were in fifth grade. I was 10 years old. I was an incredibly shy (odd?) kid, so I really didn't interact too easily with girls. Hell, I didn't even really interact too easily with boys, for that matter.

See, my single mom and two older sisters raised me to be the baby, eternally doted on and cared for by the womenfolk. As a result of that, I was naïve and pretty much sheltered from any real "coming of age" talks – no "birds and bees" talks or "this is what you have to do to be a man" talks. Indeed, the idea of my sisters or my mom having these kinds of talks with their baby brother or baby boy was profane. Therefore, I was pretty much left to think that my new sexual urges and alleged wet dreams were weird. I didn't think of them as "sinful" – we didn't have that sort of parochial thinking – but just "weird," because this was decades before Google[8] and, like many Native families, there was no man around to help me make sense of becoming a man.

Again, I was shy. Plus, even for this poor place, my family was exceptionally poor. It's nice to say that material things don't matter,

---

[8]For a person to now have the option to simply type into a computer or smartphone the question, "Are babies made by a man peeing into a woman?" seems so much more humane than having to ask an actual person. This is one of the better points about technology, in my humble opinion.

but at the time it really sucked to be wearing your sisters' hand-me-downs. Therefore, I felt inadequate and ugly – unworthy to receive attention from the cool kids of our little, Indigenous Saved by the Bell cast. I mean, lovely Lisa Turtle never flirted with Screech, did she?

Yet somehow beautiful Lydia always made me feel worthy, adequate – she helped me not to be shy. She talked to me – not really about romantic or amorous things; I wouldn't even have known what those things were. But I sensed that she enjoyed talking to me. Nobody else seemed to really enjoy talking to me, but she did.[9] She teased me. I teased her. She flirted with me. I think I may have even flirted with her. To paraphrase Edwin Arlington Robinson, "She was always human when she talked." She was sweet to everyone, but I was really the only one with whom she flirted.

Mind you, I was not an exceptional kid in too many ways. My head was larger than most of the kids in my grade. My feet were pretty big, too – my shoe size generally matched my age. But for the most part, I was just the typical, little dusty rez kid who simply wanted to watch wrestling and play basketball. Still, there was one way that I was profoundly different from every other boy in my class – unlike most of them, I didn't think that every girl in the class liked me. No, I was the exact opposite. I didn't think that any of them liked me. But... well, I thought about this a million times...and even though I'm kinda embarrassed to say this, I have to say this...

...I was pretty sure that Lydia liked me.

ACT 2
AWARENESS

May. Fifth grade. Somehow we made it through the 5th grade year in one piece. On our rez, that was never a guaranteed thing – this was an eventful year, and very much an omen of even wilder years

---

[9] I felt like Ted in Something About Mary. Ted: "I couldn't believe that she knew my name. Some of my best friends didn't know my name."

ahead. To wit, in 5th grade I (1) got jumped once by a group of kids and got my tooth knocked through my lip; on another occasion, (2) also almost lost an eye running into a barbed wire fence in the middle of the night. On yet another occasion, I (3) almost shot my uncle as I was first learning how to handle handguns. All in the 5th grade. Long and entertaining stories, definitely. Yet those are stories for another day. This story is about Lydia and how she changed how I thought when I still first learning to think. Suffice it to say that all of us little 5th graders were happy as the deep, deep snow and ice melted and the spring brought warmer weather.

It was an amazing year of growth for me. I began, ever so slightly, to begin feeling comfortable in my own skin. I found out that I was a pretty decent basketball player and could actually be funny if I didn't tense up too much.

Toward the end of the year, informed and inspired by Lydia's attention and conversation, I began hanging out with other kids more often. I actually had friends! Even more, I now had friends who invited me, an awkward, pigeon-toed kid who showered once a week, to sleep over at their houses. My mom was simultaneously sad and happy; since the death of my older brother, she loved to keep me wayyy too close to her (my sisters like to joke that I breastfed till I was 8). Yet, she understood the importance of a child's social development in theory, and so she would begrudgingly let me go.

The Oedipus complex goes strong in Indian Country – I'm pretty positive that I wasn't the only eight-year-old breastfeeder.

Nonetheless, I escaped the loving clutches of my mom to embrace this new social calendar. I became a prolific sleepover-er, staying at various friends' houses as the weather got warmer and the nights got more explorable. It was an amazing learning time. During that time, I learned the value of showering more frequently, not for the sake of hygiene, but because I didn't want my new friends making fun of my skid marks in my tighty whities. Also, we learned to navigate awkward situations; we'd all sleep in one bed – my friends were also poor – and we'd oftentimes wake up with each other's underdeveloped morning woods pressed up against each other.

Ew. "Move along, nothing to see here, folks...."

Most of our fun was extremely innocent. Fighting. Ding dong ditch. Stealing stuff. Atari. Nothing out of the ordinary – this was, after all, the place about which famed radio DJ Paul Harvey once said to go "if you wanted to get away with murder." So the stuff we were doing?? That was really tame stuff.

But then, ends of innocence happen really suddenly. JFK's assassination. MLK's assassination. The Iran hostage situation. AIDS. 9/11. They all snuck up on us – we didn't see them coming. Likewise, I surely did not see the end of my innocence coming. Not one bit. But like all of the aforementioned, it changed my life and the way that I conduct myself.

I remember it as clear as day, we were staying at my friend Dion's house – there were four of us there. Dion was the oldest and the alpha, and so he told us that we were going out that night. None of us had much parental supervision, so it was no chore to slip out that night. None of us questioned Dion – he was the Native Zach Morris – when he spoke, we listened. We walked toward our destination. Dion lived in an area unpretentiously named "Old Low Rent Project" and we quickly and stealthily made our way to the other side of town. I had the same knot in my stomach that I usually got when I was doing something that I shouldn't be doing – even though it was warm outside, I had my nervous shivers going strongly.

I didn't want to be there. I didn't know why – once again, most of our fun was extremely innocent; I had no reason to think that this would be any different. Nonetheless, I knew I didn't want to be there.

We arrived at the destination. I didn't recognize it; it was an old house that I had never been to before. It had several old cars in the front yard, and some Christmas lights strewn about. I still didn't know what was going on or why we were here – a party? A fight?

Something bad. I felt it.

Dion and the crew went around back and knocked lightly on a window. Nothing. Dion knocked again – even quieter this time. The curtains rustled. I saw eyes, and couldn't make them out at first. Then I recognized them. Lydia. Lydia looked out from her dark bedroom and she locked eyes with me. She looked shocked, and then she smiled. I smiled too – I was happy to see her. She opened the window and whispered, "I didn't know that you were coming."

I tried to play cool and make my squeaky voice less squeaky, "Yeah, I wanted to!" All four of us crawled in the window and obviously were as quiet as we could be...the lights remained off.

She whispered, "You ready?" There was no verbal response from Dion (or anybody else), but instead the sounds of a zipper opening and quick squeaks of the box springs. It finally dawned on me why we were here. It was inelegant and awkward – no kissing, no talking – instead, one by one, Lydia took turns having sex with each of my friends. Along with the squeaking I could barely hear, in the background, the sound of the TV playing the theme from Three's Company. There were no screams like I had seen in movies. There were no condoms (although I probably wouldn't even have known what a condom was at that time); there were no precautions. Honestly, I wanted to throw up. But I didn't. I didn't make a sound – I hoped that they didn't remember I was there.

They either forgot about me or didn't care that I never took my turn. I don't know which it was. All I know is that I did not participate and instead sat crying in the dark like a freakin' baby. Fortunately there were enough people in the room and it was dark enough that my bawling on the floor (and not participating) wasn't obvious. I probably wanted to participate, but my heart was too busy being broken. In hindsight, I'm profoundly glad that I didn't, but as with most things in life it wasn't so clear-cut at the time.

I couldn't participate, even though it was disgustingly erotic.

Lydia wasn't guarded like I thought a 10-year-old girl should have been. Her parents were in the other room and couldn't hear anything because their TV was on. Hell, we weren't guarded like 10-year-old boys should have been. Nobody ever asked about that night, or the many other nights we snuck out. Nobody ever noticed.

I don't think Lydia and I ever spoke again after that night, even though I saw her plenty of times. She is a beautiful mother, and actually a grandmother now. I sometimes see her and her husband in the grocery store, pushing their shopping cart together – she looked great, like it wasn't nearly as traumatic an experience for her as it was for me. It definitely didn't seem like that unfortunate night defined her future relationships with men – she and her husband looked like they had a sweet and healthy relationship. I convince myself that she and I both recovered from that night. Maybe I'm just overly sensitive? I am a mama's boy, after all. In either event, it took me another eight years to finally have my first kiss. In the same way that night didn't seem to define Lydia's future relationships with men, I want to believe it didn't define my interactions or relationships with women.

ACT 3
POSTSCRIPT

The moral of the story? Meh...I'm not big into morals. The experience kinda was what it was – heartbreaking, erotic and prescient all at the same time. This story isn't about morals though; this story is about saying thank you to Lydia.

My mom had her first child at 14. A boy. My oldest brother. He died when I was a little kid.

I worshipped my sisters and mom so I would have never, ever realized the difficulty that they had being kids with kids. They were superwomen – they made it look easy. Lydia was different. When I saw her just a few years after that night towing her beautiful little brown baby around, I remembered how free she was that night in the house, and I instantly equated "sex" with "babies" and "responsibility." I also started to associate easy sex with fatherless children like me and all of my buddies running through the reservation at night.

I didn't want to be that kind of dad.

In hindsight, I know that many reservation issues are structural. Our homelands were designed to struggle economically. It's part of the larger American economic plan – economic struggle creates social problems. That's proven – most marriages end because of money problems, and since reservations tend to have very serious money problems, it stands to reason that the family unit struggles on-reservation. As my conspiracy-minded dad would've said, "The man wants us to fail!" Yet, despite those structural problems, we have an obligation to protect the Lydias of the world. Lydia was not an anomaly, and neither were the young boys who had sex with her. Therein lies our culpability. It was not that Lydia's parents were bad. She got good grades, was well-dressed, was always in school, etc. It's just that, like most parents, they were distracted.

That's true with Native and non-Native parents alike, parents are distracted. However, it's especially true in places where parents have to search high and low for resources to try to keep the lights on and food on the table.

That night taught me that I have a duty to make sure that my kids, nieces, and nephews are well-informed and ready to deal with the consequences of their actions. Reckoning with the experience taught me that our young folks – girls and boys – need demonstrations of healthy love, not scalding judgment and disengagement. Native people, by the benign economic, political and educational neglect that we find within our communities, are taught that any attention is good attention. That's what Lydia thought. That's what all of us believed. That is also what we have the potential to change.

We have to take care of the things that we can take care of. We've got to take care of home. We can literally change the world one kid at a time if we just invest the time and love to do it.

Lydia should have been protected. My friends and I should have been protected. Strong Native love should protect our young ones from these sorts of experiences. A strong love that checks what our kids are doing at night, doesn't let them lock their doors with butter knives, and demands answers to awkward questions. From that night in that room, I learned that I have to do my small part to make sure our people and our families are protected. Our communal history, and my personal experience, has shown me that no one has, or will, protect and value the lives of our children for us.

(This story is, of course, for "Lydia" and the generations of unsupervised kids, Native and non, boys and girls. As parents, we now have an opportunity to change history for our kids.)

NIANKHKHNUM

It was a beautiful early evening
Perfect day for love.

Summertime was gorgeous
80 degrees
A long romantic walk
Young happy couple
Enjoying the cool relief of the breeze.

Everybody was taking a walk tonight.
Their body language changed and they stopped laughing.

They knew exactly what was coming
Saw the aggressive gaze out of the corners of their eyes
Crazed looks combined with groupthink
Yet
It was just a group of guys passing another couple of guys.
On the surface it seemed innocuous
Three long-haired Native men
Passed two short-haired Native men without exchanging head nods
or "hi's"
No overt acknowledgment
Yet
That really should not have been a big surprise.

Really,
That wasn't unusual
Men of color being standoffish with each other happened everywhere
Still the short-haired men glanced back suspiciously
Something told them that they better stay aware
They were used to the jokes
Young men teasing them about the highlights in their hair
The snug shirts and the white belts
The loafers and cologne that they wear
"Nobody wears that shit around here."
Young men were entertained by the pair

Laughing at the high-pitched tone of the two men's giggles
Most of the time the couple didn't seem to even care
They knew it came with the territory
Made a choice to stay home
Despite the suspicious glares
Had to be near their families
Wasn't even an option to walk around scared
This was where they're from
Dammit
They couldn't care less who stared!
The shorter one had his cell phone open
Just in case – couldn't be too prepared

Then the larger one squeezed his hand tighter
Looked his partner in the eyes and smiled.

Then they relaxed a bit
The shorter one said, "You're right. I'm overreacting."
The couple looked back and the three young men disappeared
The couple looked at each other and exhaled
As if they knew that there was no reason for fear
What happened in the city was in the city
Where people said that it was supposed to be safe to be a queer
But the assault came so unexpectedly and brutally
While being publicly affectionate on the eve of the New Year
Plastic surgery
Not for vanity
But because the beating was so severe
Had to move near his family to recover
It took him a full year.
But there hasn't even been the slightest little incident here.
Other than a few stares.

Then the taller one said to his dearest love
"Even though they don't understand us
Our people do understand loving through pain
Loving to the point where you should give it up
Where the love seems to be in vain
But still you keep going back

Causes you to question whether loves makes you insane
We should have quit each other after that night
Hell
I would have quit men altogether if I had half a brain
But I choose to love you like an Indian
Because desperate love runs deep in our veins
And they understand that.
Even if they don't understand us
This is home
And they respect our love
And our willingness to die for our love
Like our ancestors before us
Where the warriors set up war camps far away from the village so
that the carnage never
Touches the family
And they could die alone if there was dying to be done.
But the community could go on.
And as long as they understand that
We'll never have to worry."

(This story is for TJ and James, Jeremy and Jake and the Suquamish Tribe – for showing the power a community can hold to make its members feel safe and wanted.)

ABOUT THE COVER

A young Blackfeet beauty named Daisy Norris or "Dawn Mist" inspired the cover. She typified Native love for her people, for women, and for her family. The non-Native residents who visited the camps in Blackfeet Country in Glacier Park were taken with Daisy's beauty and gave her the title "Dawn Mist" as a form of honor. She was a social progressive in the early 20th century – working for women's suffrage and for women to be treated equally in work environments; she later married Bill Gilham. Bill and Daisy's love created a powerful bond that produced five Blackfeet boys who all fought in World War II and were, like their mother, renowned for being exceptionally attractive. Daisy was well-documented – photographed many, many times over and painted many times as well, including reportedly being painted by Winold Reiss. Newspapers across the country ran pictures of her and it is safe to say that her beauty was transcendent. This book's cover image is breathtaking and the photograph inspired us to learn a bit more about an inspirational woman and I thank Fredricka, Toni and everybody else who helped us in this endeavor to learn more about her.

ABOUT THE AUTHOR
NATIVE PEOPLE MAKE THE BEST LOVERS

Photo courtesy of Martin Sensmeier

Gyasi Ross is a member of the Blackfeet Nation; he resides on and also comes from the Suquamish Nation on the Port Madison Indian Reservation. Both are his Homelands and he loves being in his Homelands. He is a father to an amazing and rotten little boy, an author who writes for online and print publications and also writes books and sometimes bad comedy. He is also a lawyer and a filmmaker. Most of all, he is a storyteller and comes from a long line of storytellers.

His Blackfoot name is Oonikoomsika. He tries to live up to his name.

He used to think that he wanted to be a politician or to have a long and illustrious career as a lawyer and that would be the way that he would affect the most positive change. But he realized that the problems in the world aren't related to laws or politics – they're related to love. We don't love ourselves or our communities anymore – as a result, we simply do not invest in them. Now, he's moved away from the law and the politics and he's pretty certain that his Creator simply put him on Mother Earth for two things: to be a responsible parent, and to tell stories the best he can. Native people have the best love stories – they simply haven't been told to the public at large. In this age of excess and materialism, the world needs those stories of love when loving seemed impossible and futile and when investment usually didn't come with a return. Altruistic love, with no guarantee of yield – that kind of love is powerful.

That is Native love.

Once those beautiful stories get out there – once people hear about Native peoples' love affair with the Earth and living in balance with all living beings – all people will want a piece of it. How could they not?? This book is simply a small first step, to introduce the world to the notion that Native people – those stoic, serious and buckskinned people of Edward C. Curtis photos – love and love deeply. Native peoples' brand of love is undying and powerful and painful. It endures and continues without entitlement.

The world can learn something from that type of love.